Advance Praise for *Johnny Cash and the Great American Contradiction*

"Reading this book is like taking a road trip across the United States with a smart, faithful, sympathetic, and keen-eyed buddy. We encounter Johnny Cash, Sister Rosetta Tharpe, low-fat foods, bumper stickers, Marvin Gaye, TV westerns, *Moby Dick*, and Martin Luther King Jr., all through the lens of a theologically sophisticated Christian faith. Rodney Clapp challenges Christians to see the importance of the church of Jesus Christ as mediating between God and America. And, in doing so, he shows once again that sound theology that is accessible and relevant to popular culture is not a contradiction in terms."

—William Cavanaugh, Associate Professor of Theology, University of St. Thomas, Saint Paul, Minnesota

"With captivating prose and illuminating analogies, Rodney Clapp draws on Christian conviction, the Man in Black, and an impressive array of poets, musicians, and writers to explore some of the enduring tensions that lie at the heart of the American experiment. His insightful analysis of country music is matched by an equally incisive analysis of political trends and cultural contradictions. And he brings to this work his usual keen understanding of church and culture. Importantly, at this moment in our nation's history, Clapp shows us that it's possible to be a faithful Christian and a true patriot at the same time. Along the way, we have the great pleasure of seeing how the life and music of Johnny Cash were informed by his Christian faith and his American patriotism."

—Kristen Deede Johnson, Associate Director of the CrossRoads Project, Director of the Studies in Ministry Minor, and Assistant Professor of Political Science, Hope College, Holland, Michigan

D0290138

Johnny Cash and the
Great American Contradiction

Johnny Cash and the
Great American Contradiction

CHRISTIANITY AND THE
BATTLE FOR THE SOUL OF A NATION

Rodney Clapp

Westminster John Knox Press
LOUISVILLE • LONDON

Scripture quotations from the New Revised Standard Version of the Bible are copyright © 1989 by the Division of Christian Education of the National Council of the Churches of Christ in the U.S.A. and are used by permission.

Book design by Sharon Adams
Cover design by designpointinc.com

First edition
Published by Westminster John Knox Press
Louisville, Kentucky

This book is printed on acid-free paper that meets the American National Standards Institute Z39.48 standard. ∞

PRINTED IN THE UNITED STATES OF AMERICA

08 09 10 11 12 13 14 15 16 17 — 10 9 8 7 6 5 4 3 2 1

Library of Congress Cataloging-in-Publication Data

Clapp, Rodney.
    Johnny Cash and the great American contradiction : Christianity and the battle for the soul of a nation / Rodney Clapp. — 1st ed.
        p. cm.
    Includes index.
    ISBN 978-0-664-23088-3 (alk. paper)
        1. Christianity and culture—United States. 2. United States—Church history. 3. Cash, Johnny. I. Title.

BR515.C528 2008
261.0973—dc22

2007039283

To
B. J. Heyboer, admired colleague and
devotee extraordinaire of Johnny Cash,
and
Stanley Hauerwas, who never stops giving and
speaks with a pronounced southern accent

Contents

Introduction

This Turbulent American Moment and the Fifth Face on Mt. Rushmore

*T*he United States of America has been called the Great Experiment—a noble, daring, open-ended laboratory of democracy and freedom. It certainly is noble and brave. But one of the things that makes the American Experiment threatening as well as inspiring, frustrating as well as fascinating, is the series of contradictions at its heart, and still pulsing through its bloodstream today. America says all "men" are created free and equal, but it was a slaveholder who penned that great dictum of the national creed. America is a republic founded on capitalism, but strives to be a democracy, governed "by the people," and not a plutocracy, ruled by the wealthy. America is at once the vanguard modern, secular nation and, by its citizens' professions of faith, the most religious country in the "developed" world. Yet again, America assumes the dirty-handed, death-dealing burdens of empire but still imagines itself a nation of exceptional innocence. Consider one last contradiction. America assumed itself to be breaking away from the vicious, mired circle of hateful memories and violence consuming the Old World; but America itself harbors destructive myths of the effectiveness of violence and revenge that leave it, in fact, the most violent country in the postindustrial world

Especially since September 11, 2001, it has been difficult to openly acknowledge and grapple with these central contradictions in our national character. There were early hopes that a unifying response to the midnight-dark catastrophe of that day would draw a huge and hugely diverse nation together. Those hopes evaporated quickly. Osama Bin Laden succeeded all too completely in making Americans desperately and destructively afraid. We not only became aware and understandably fearful of the potential for acts of terrorism on our soil, but became hateful and afraid of fellow Americans in a way we were not before. Our own ruling party soon decided that heightening fear and polarizing the citizenry was politically expedient. (As journalist Ron Suskind reports, the intelligence community was aware as early as 2004 that the Bush administration knew "that when the al Qaeda leader displays his forceful presence, [President Bush's] own approval ratings rise, and vice versa.")[1] Americanism was defined in absolutistic, even religious terms, excluding national self-criticism, narrowing the parameters of debate, and sowing suspicion of those citizens who did not hold the regnant political and militaristic views. For some of us, this sorry situation has raised a real and pressing question: Can someone be both a conscientious Christian and a loyal American?

Like millions of other Americans, by the winter and spring of 2002 I found myself less at ease than before with an array of family, friends, and fellow churchgoers. We were certainly previously aware of differences between ourselves. But cultural turbulence, stark political division, media hysteria, and anger meant that we could no longer speak freely or reasonably about what our country was doing and where it was going. It is painful, as so many of us have learned—on whatever side of the political divide—when talking about urgent matters with longtime friends, to find yourself hedging, probing, pulling back at the first sign of strain, and finally simply trying to steer conversation to less passionate (and less important) ground. It has been easiest, by far, to watch, read, and listen to the media and personalities that agree with "my side" of the issues, and ignore or flail wildly at others. For those of us who are active worshipers as well as Americans, this polarization has been doubly painful. We are divided not only as a nation but as communities of faith. The United States, which has never been an officially Christian nation, is now closer to that status than at any time in its history. As the Republican Party platforms in Texas, Arizona, and other states expressly indicate, many American Christians think America as a Christian nation is a fine and even necessary idea.[2]

I am among those Christians who think this is a bad idea, not just or even primarily for the nation, but for the church. Designating a nation-state as the community of mission serving the God met in Jesus Christ is theologically disastrous. It is theologically disastrous because no nation past or present can share the unique chosen status granted Israel in the biblical story, and because Christ and the apostles named the Israel-born church as their community of mission to and in the world. No other community or political entity need apply.

Mistaking and misnaming the community of Christian proclamation and service to the world—as America or as any other national claimant to the title—then radically distorts Christian mission. In fact, such a confused categorization is not so much Christian mission as Christian dis-mission. It dismisses the church from its proper identity, service, and role on earth. And in the process it makes America assume an identity and role that no nation-state should assume, and can assume only to its detriment. It is no favor to a carpenter to assign the carpenter the role and work of a tailor. Such misnaming results only in beleaguered carpenters and unwearable clothes. Likewise, mistaking America for the church results in a frustrated nation and an insufferable religion. People of other faiths in America and around the world are already frightened and angered at such a prospect. Many—but by no means all—Christians also see the problem. What could be more dangerous than a nation that is by far the most overwhelming military and economic power in history *and* thinks it is a church righteously responsible for the salvation of the world?

In these pages, then, I want to wrestle with what it means to be a Christian and an American, in the truest and best sense of both words. While I emphatically do not believe America is or should be a Christian nation, I affirm that America's history and the current composition of its citizenry (Christian of one stripe or another by a large majority) mean that Christianity (and other religions, especially Judaism) cannot be simply ignored in the public square. It is exactly a better understanding of Christian convictions and practices that will help all Christians appreciate why America should not strive for the status of "Christian nation." Positively, the church needs to sort out ways in which it is itself truly and appropriately "public" and "political," and to ask what are its genuine responsibilities to and for the world. More specifically, at this troubled hour, those of us who live and worship in the United States might helpfully work at what we can do to support America exactly as Christians. It is precisely distinctively Christian convictions and practices that can better help a confused, angry, and afraid America to sort out what it is and what it is about. And it is exactly at the raw node of its deepest contradictions that the country might gain clarification and perhaps some hope from the church.

That is true because America's aspirations have been and now are again outrightly theological, and thus must be addressed theologically. It is also true because Christians are people who must learn to live amid tensions and with contradictions. We are after all a people who profess that in Christ the kingdom of God has already arrived on earth, but is not yet here in all its fullness. Christians dwell between the old age of grievous division and a new age of wonderful reconciliation. We worship a God who is both three and one, and follow a Savior whom we know as fully human and fully divine. Our tradition teaches us that these are not brute or final contradictions, but that only God can experience and know these realities comprehensively, see the entire picture at once. At the human, limited, creaturely level we cannot help but know aspects of our lives and our witness as in tension and some degree of practical contradiction. Accordingly, Christian reflection and spirituality is marinated in contradictions—practically and immediately, if not logically and ultimately.[3] My hunch is that this vantage point and training can illuminate the present predicament of the Great Contradiction that is America. In some cases, such attention may show contradictions to be merely apparent, and therefore temporary and solvable. In others, it may show them to be irresolvable, but they will surely be better endured by a keener understanding of them and their irresolvability.

⚜⚜⚜⚜⚜⚜⚜

In this brief book, I will focus on the contradictions I have already hinted at in the very beginning of this introduction. These are America's simultaneous embrace of holiness and hedonism, its pining love of tradition as it carries on a headlong romantic affair with progress, its extreme individualism coursing beside a gigantic, gaping yearning for community, and its insistence on innocence at the same time it revels in violence. I will gnaw at the marrows of these American bones—bones of contention as well as bones of strength and stature—through attention to a particular, and originally southern, culture: that of country music. More specifically, I will focus especially on a single country musician, Johnny Cash.

There are limitations to reading or reflecting on a reality as large and varied as the United States through any one figure. Obviously, this book is no attempt at a final or ultimately comprehensive rendering of America and American possibilities as we now know them. Shortly, I will elaborate on the specifics that make Cash's life and work widely illuminating. But first it may help to consider how country music—the central concern of Cash's life and work—can reveal characteristics of all of America, not simply one region or a narrow "ghetto" of American rednecks.

In this regard, it is important to dispense with misconceptions that country music appeals only to rural Americans, especially at a time when only 20 percent of our citizens reside in rural areas.[4] Certainly the music has rural and southern roots, but then so do millions of Americans now living in surburban or urban settings. No small number have taken with them their love of country music, as is evidenced by radio station demographics. Country music is in fact the most widely popular radio format in the nation, with 2,028 stations devoted to the genre. (The nearest competitor is talk radio, with 1,318 stations; the closest musical challenger is that of "oldies," at 793 stations. Top 40, urban, and rock music formats, despite their higher profiles, all lag far behind.)[5] So country music reflects not only the southern values of significant concern in this book, but those perspectives and attitudes aired throughout the nation, and demographically more pervasive in city settings than rural.

Appropriately to the linguistic medium of books, and this particular book's discussion, country music centers on its lyrics. Jazz and classical music are fundamentally instrumental, and in all events draw fewer listeners than country. Rock music's recorded or live sound mixes frequently subordinate vocals to electric guitars and percussion. For country music, the vocalist's words and intonations are paramount. Even rap, which certainly puts a premium on lyrical invention, is mixed so that bass lines and percussion often over-shadow and obscure the rapper's words. (And rap appeals to a tighter age demographic than country.) If there is a practice of poetry still heard by a wide swath of Americans on an everyday and popular level, it is that of country music. More directly to the point, country's lyrical content broadly if not universally encompasses the key American thematic contradictions I am concerned to address. As the genre's foremost historian, Bill Malone, argues, "[I]t is the tensions and conflicting postures found in this great music, and not its alleged simplicity, that make it eternally appealing." So it is that country singers and songwriters "deal constantly" with such "warring impulses as piety and hedonism, home and rambling, companionship and individualism, and nostalgia and modernity"—exactly the sorts of national contradictions over which we will here linger.[6]

Finally, in its performative intent as well as its lyrical content, country music consistently focuses on democratic ideals and realities, another key theme of this book. Country music makes no pretense of appealing to other than "ordinary" people or "plain folk." Listeners identify with country music artists as "one of us." So country artists markedly do not flaunt their wealth ("bling" will not advance their careers or images) and routinely insist that their celebrity has not separated them from their rustic origins. Country music recording companies, unlike those in any other genre, expect even the most successful artists to spend entire workdays signing autographs and shaking hands with fans.[7]

All that said on behalf of country's broad representation, my deepest concern with the music's cultural limitations is its lingering and often proud provincialism. No other contemporary musical culture would so successfully and uncritically adore such jingoistic anthems as Lee Greenwood's "God Bless the U.S.A." And certainly the most aggressively chauvinistic popular music in response to the tragedy of 9/11 has been made by country artists such as Toby Keith. Perhaps even more significantly, though country music enjoys a surprising number of African American fans, prominent black and other minority performers are conspicuously scarce in the music.[8]

Besides supporting a wider racial and political base for the music, my basic response to the provincialism of country music culture is to surface and highlight the actual, if obscured, diversity inherent to the culture. We may at least remember the black musicians who have (albeit all too covertly) contributed to the birth and growth of country music. To take but three prominent examples: Country pioneer A. P. Carter had no skill in musical notation and no ear for remembering the vast number of melodies collected on song-foraging expeditions through the Appalachian hills and valleys. His indispensable collecting partner, then, was the African American guitarist Lesley Riddle, who accompanied Carter on his rambles. Hank Williams learned guitar from (black) Alabama street musician Rufus Payne (known as "Tee-Tot"). And a young Johnny Cash honed his abilities and learned the rudiments of his signature sound when, as a frustrated door-to-door appliance salesman, he repeatedly set aside all patter about washing machines or refrigerators and took up his guitar with residents on the porches of black neighborhoods in Memphis.

More generally, country music culture, like almost any culture of some duration, is indelibly marked by borrowings and adaptations from other cultures. The fiddle is a European instrument. The banjo has African origins. The steel guitar, a hallmark of the country sound, came not from Kentucky or Tennessee, but from the nineteenth-century Hawaiian Islands. Square dancing has its roots in the old aristocracy of France, which explains why even callers who insist on ordering freedom fries at a restaurant speak French ("allemande," "promenade," "chassez/sashay") on the dance floor. Yodeling? Nineteenth-century American cowpokes knew nothing of it. This vocal flourish was introduced to America by touring German choral groups and was first practiced by cowboys on the western "ranches" of 1930s Hollywood movie sets. On these and many other counts, the culture of country music is not as insular and provincial as its detractors think—or as it may imagine itself to be.

⭐⭐⭐⭐⭐⭐⭐

To bring an even sharper focus to America's great democracy and its great contradictions, I will, as I have said, concentrate on a single country music artist, Johnny Cash. In fact, a reflection on American character could hardly have a more justifiable subject for its focus. Very few figures in recent history are seen as more representative of American identity than Cash. His music was included in a space capsule the United States shot into outer space. He played Abraham Lincoln in a television miniseries and was a major player in the celebration of the country's bicentennial. His has often been suggested as the face that should be added to the select pantheon on Mt. Rushmore.[9] But in addition to his profound Americanness, the late and still celebrated country singer and songwriter, in his life and work, provides several lamps to shine into the neglected, shadowy twists and crevices of the caverns of America's current religious, cultural, and political predicaments.

Johnny Cash was a lifelong Christian. Raised in the Baptist church, particularly impressed by his mother (who sometimes baked "Scripture cakes" using ingredients listed in the Bible), Cash held deep Christian convictions from childhood to his death. Like America in general and the South in particular, he was God-haunted. He did not always live up to his convictions but, even at his drug-addled and beastly worst, he never relinquished them. Christian convictions and practices profoundly mark his work, which still rings out across the country and the world—in radio, films, and television commercials. Cash's famous sympathy for the outsider and the underdog, represented through frequent prison concerts and his customary funereal black attire, sprang from the soil of faith. In the turbulent late sixties and early seventies, some accused him of becoming a "political radical." Cash responded, "I'm just trying to be a Christian." On another occasion he elaborated, "As I got to studying the Bible more, I found it part of my religion, not only an obligation but a privilege, to perform for people in bondage, especially those behind bars."[10] Like America as a whole, Cash had a sometimes constructive and sometimes tortured relation to the church and the faith. He and his music can help us see more keenly into the often baffling murkiness that is the American relation between holiness and hedonism, church and state, faith and culture.

The Man in Black's solidarity with the poor, the imprisoned, and the overburdened working people tapped into his Christian faith. It also reflected what many of us continue to regard as among America's greatest ideals and real if fragmentary glories. Cash was thoroughly an American proud of the Americanness represented by Emma Lazurus's words inscribed at the base of the Statue of Liberty, also known as the "Mother of Exiles":

> Give me your tired, your poor,
> Your huddled masses yearning to breathe free,
> The wretched refuse of your teeming shore,
> Send these, the homeless, tempest-tost to me,
> I lift my lamp beside the golden door!

Such sympathies entailed that Cash was not blind to the imperfections of his native land. Paired with his patriotism and a number of traits native to his rural southern home, these sympathies meant Cash's Americanism was too broad and too deep to stand on only one side of our current red state vs. blue state polarization. Like other southerners, if not always in identical regards, Cash was pleased to be known as a rebel—a rebel, as he once put it, "against a stagnant status quo, against our hypocritical houses of God, against people whose minds are closed to others' ideas."[11] At the same time, like others of his vintage, he could not conceive of anything but standing for his country on the whole, and when push came to shove.

Born in 1932, Cash came of age with generations who saw the nation through the Depression, the Dust Bowl, and World War II. He recorded entire albums of patriotic songs and was ill at ease with protestors of the Vietnam war. His typically straightforward assessment: "I think everybody should serve their time for their country. I did. It's not up to every man to decide when it's time to defend our country. We elect men to decide that for us."[12] Civil rights battles, Vietnam, and Watergate would complicate such absolute patriotism for Cash, as for other Americans.[13] Of course, the man was not a politician or political theorist, so what we are talking about are not systematic reflections but honest sentiments. Those sentiments were bone-deep and defining for Cash's identity. In a 1971 interview, June Carter Cash blurted, "John has never believed in war. I don't think anybody does. But you know, if you don't stand for your country . . . I don't know . . . you've got to believe in the principles this country stands for."[14] I suspect Johnny shared the ambivalence and confusion reflected in his beloved spouse's stuttering, stumbling statement. She and he sensed national faultlines at a tectonic level, yet to imagine an identity and responsibility not fundamentally American was impossible. Any glimmering of such an alternative could only trail off and fade beyond the horizon of articulation. Johnny Cash's profoundly American identity can help us probe into and onto the obscured ledges of American characteristics and their limitations no less than their merits.

But with all this said, Johnny Cash was first and foremost a country music singer and songwriter. This is why we all know him and will remember his name. He was an incarnate repository and transmitter of the American musical heritage. In a sense, all native American music is southern, with the blues-based musics of jazz, country, and rock flowing out of the Mississippi Delta and flooding the entire world. Cash grew up barely forty miles from Memphis, its ancient Egyptian name apropos to that city's unquestionable status as the Rosetta Stone of popular American music. Cash possessed an encyclopedic recall of hundreds if not thousands of songs of American folk origin. Through June Carter Cash, and later by incorporating not only her but Mother Maybelle into his regular stage show, he was bonded to the Carter Family. Among the very first practitioners of what came to be called country music, the Carters built their repertoire by husband/father A.P.'s already mentioned song-collecting rambles through the Appalachians in the early twentieth century. The Carter family rescued for posterity mountain and backcountry songs of Scottish and Irish descent that had been sung for generations, and reveal so much about the taproots of America's contradictory character. Among musicians, Cash is second only to Bob Dylan as an intuitive preserver and extensive popularizer of American roots music. Hear, then, Dylan's resounding testimony to Cash's artistry: "Johnny didn't have a piercing yell, but ten thousand years of culture fell from him. He could have been a cave dweller. He sounds like he's at the edge of the fire, or in the deep snow, or in a ghostly forest, the coolness of conscious obvious strength, full tilt and vibrant with danger. . . . Johnny's voice was so big, it made the world grow small."[15]

There is a final reason for using Johnny Cash as a lens through which to view American contradictions and challenges. Cash was a southerner, and to understand early-twenty-first-century America in the slightest requires understanding the American South. Born and reared in Arkansas, achieving fame in Memphis, and living the longer part of his life in Nashville, Cash imbibed the traits of the region. He loved dramatic flair (witness again the black costuming, as well as album covers depicting him as a grizzled gunfighter and a bedraggled half-Indian). He had a great gift for primal, elemental rhetoric. I remember the first time—in a dusty Oklahoma barn, milking a cow and batting away flies and her swatting tail, as I listened to a cob-webbed radio—I heard the searing declamation, "I shot a man in Reno, / just to watch him die."[16] The stark, naturalistic poetry of "I Walk the Line," "Big River," "Flesh and Blood," and a score of other classic Cash songs exemplifies his rhetorical abilities.[17] Like so many writers, orators, and musicians hailing from the South, Cash was a consummate storyteller. He venerated mama and bowed at the pedestal of the female gender. He loved his country and yet could spit at it in anger. Like a true southerner, he was God-sworn and never entirely out from under the shadow of Christ's cross. Like many southerners, Cash enjoyed guns (he owned an extensive collection). At times, bearing the imprint of a southern code going back to colonial days, he linked male honor and courage to a willingness to engage in physical violence. And obviously Cash's southern biography, if his songs less explicitly, hooks into our country's formative and ongoing trauma of racism and racial oppression.

The entire nation's culture and, particularly since the 1980s, its politics are imprinted by the American South. There is no under-standing America and its contradictions without understanding the South, and again Cash's life and work provides an excellent point of entry. Looking for Cash's America, then, we now turn toward Dixie.

Chapter 1

America's Southern Accent

*F*or his final album of the twentieth century, *Unchained,* Johnny Cash was backed by rockers Tom Petty and the Heartbreakers. Cash covered Petty's 1985 song "Southern Accents."[1] No doubt the Arkansan (Cash) and the Floridian (Petty) connected across the generational divide out of musical affinities and, as this tune evidences, out of a shared southern heritage. Cash's rendition lends an already impressive song weight and depth. His voice is aged and paradoxically strong, the baritone plunging to a bass hum at line endings, creaking not weakly but powerfully, like an oak swaying majestically in the wind. Cash's force-of-nature vocal is accompanied at first only by acoustic guitar, but not far in, Benmont Tench's organ begins to wend and twirl in and above the song, eventually unfurling like a flag or the tail of a kite. It takes the song to church and lends a sacred aura to Cash's already sepulchral intonations.

With this anointing, Petty's ballad conveys the defining and encompassing power of southern identity in the late twentieth century. Like a Mississippi River of the soul, the undertow and currents of southern character carry along all aspects of the identities of its native sons and daughters. In the South, Petty and Cash tell us, not only talking but work, prayer, and living in general are done with "a southern accent." The young ones may consider it "country," and the Yankees "call it dumb," but now southern identity, like the Mississippi in flood, has surged well beyond the banks of the South as a region. In so much of its culture, religion, politics, and society, all of America now speaks with a southern accent.

1

※※※※※※

The South did not lose the Civil War. We cannot begin to understand the current American polarization, the intensity and complexity and ambivalence of its cultural and political wars, without understanding this. Of course the South lost the war militarily—General Lee surrendered and disbanded his troops. Of course the United States of America remained a single republic (it was in fact after the Civil War that the country was referred to in the singular: "the United States *is* . . ." rather than the grammatically correct "the United States *are* . . .). Of course the institution of slavery was abolished. In these and other hugely significant regards, the South lost the Civil War.

But in many key regards, the South did not lose. It never relinquished several of its most preciously held ideals and aspirations. And in the latter half of the twentieth century and first years of the twenty-first century, it has seen many of the seeds it fought for in the nineteenth century come to flower across the nation. Consider the resurgence of the rhetoric and activism for states' rights in the last three decades. Consider how the South, long and still the most hawkish region in the country, has influenced American military involvements. Consider the domination of southern politicians and attitudes in national government, in its legislative and especially its executive branches.

The strongly southern accent or inflection of democracy as we now know it in the United States may helpfully be discerned by way of contrast. By way of broad and rough contrast, I want to suggest that American democracy is composed of two dominant strains: the democracy of the parade, based predominantly in the North; and the democracy of the revival, predominantly of the South.

New England or Yankee democracy, while certainly marked by individualism, had at its heart the practice and memories of democracy exemplified by the town meeting. The public gathered to work corporately, as a group, on its pressing public issues. If we think, roughly, of Yankee democracy as that captured by the New Yorker Walt Whitman, American democracy is a parade.[2]

The "blab of the pave," the passing rush of feet of all kinds of people, intoxicates the poet Whitman in his masterwork, *Leaves of*

Grass.[3] In a rapture, he is jostled "through streets and halls" by the vast variety of Americans who tramp with him on a "perpetual journey." His ongoing, celebratory march crosses generations and genders. It incorporates "old and young," "sweethearts and old maids," hairy-chested blacksmiths, the living child wondering at blades of grass and the dead resting beneath their "uncut hair of graves." It juxtaposes contrasting types such as the badged policeman and the manacled criminal, the runaway slave and the slavemaster, the soldier and the pacifistic Quaker, the mutineer and the ship's captain, the opium addict and the president surrounded by his cabinet. It excludes no class, proceeding with the aristocratic ballroom dancer alongside the "woollypates" who hoe cottonfields, and representing alike occupations "high" and "low"—physicians, farmers, mechanics, lawyers, sailors, trappers, priests, firemen, prostitutes, peddlers, photographers. It knows no respect of race, bringing in its tow the "negro from Africa" and the "Mexican native" no less than the Anglo Yankee; the Eskimo dwelling in a "dark cold snowhouse" no less than the "Chinese with his transverse eyes"; the "red squaw" no less than the white congressman. It includes losers as well as winners: "I play not a march for victors only. . . . I play great marches / for conquered and slain persons." Here come together people from red state and blue state both: Hoosier, Badger, Buckeye, Louisianian, Georgian, "Utahian," "Kansian," "Arkansian," the citizen from the "hills of Vermont" with the woodsman from Maine and the rancher from Texas.

Whitman's democracy revels in differences ("I resist anything better than my own diversity") and is indeed nothing so much as a sometimes wild and conflictual parade, maintaining a "place" for each and for all.

> Each has his own place in the procession.
> All is a procession,
> The universe is a procession with measured and beautiful motion.

So this democracy is not a mere concatenation of self-interested differences, with races and occupations and classes careening randomly like billiard balls, smacking accidentally into one other and flying in opposite directions. It really is a parade, headed in a shared and common direction. The parts may be atomistic but, in Whitman's estimate, they relate: "For every atom belonging to me as good as belongs to you." So these parts are best known not separately and in isolation, but in their relations one to another within the whole. Americans know themselves most truly as Americans not in their individualistic hermitages, but when they gather and join the great national parade of democracy.

Democracy with a southern accent, on the other hand, is not so much a parade marked by corporate similarities and shared destinations. The intrepid early immigrants to what would come to be known as New England came ashore in united boatloads, in bodies of several families that imagined themselves linked in a commonwealth, a polity, from the very start.[4] Such a spirit, as I have remarked, continued in the town meetings and goes on in memory and practice today. The southern immigrants, by contrast, spread more slowly and gradually over a (much more vast) region. They immigrated not as already existing communities or nascent polities, but as single men or isolated families. Thus a frontier spirit of competition and self-reliance imprinted southern democracy. The heavily Scotch and Irish ancestry of southern white settlers may have borne stronger independent streaks than other Europeans—the Scots and Irish hailed from borderlands trying violently to break free of English sway long before they came to American shores. However much we should make of their ancestral temperament, white southerners were spread over a much more sparsely populated region than New Englanders, one which urbanized much later, one where rural planters and craftsmen and farmers emphasized their comparative self-sufficiency. As the southern chronicler W. J. Cash observed, the plantation existed as an independent social unit, a "little world of its own." And a fierce spirit of atomistic individualism was true not only for plantation masters but for poor whites, who were "as jealous of their sway over their puny domains, as the grandest lord."[5] A southern aversion to taxation (with or without "representation") and other manifestations of centralized authority well predates the American Revolution.

The democracy more characteristic of the South, I want to suggest, is accordingly not so much that of the parade as that of the revival. The evangelicalism of the South was solidified with the Second and

Third Great Awakenings (in the 1800s–1830s and 1880s–1900s). In the twentieth century North Carolina native Billy Graham would spread southern revivalism and evangelicalism to California and eventually across the nation, helped not least by the Southern Baptist Convention, which is today the largest Protestant denomination in America. There is much to be said about revivalistic Christianity, but my point is simple: revivalism nurtured a democracy more individualistic and more insular than Whitman's democratic parade.[6]

The revival, to be sure, is a corporate gathering. But it is not as diverse in composition as the Whitmanian democratic parade. Obviously, it does not reach beyond those who will affirm the Christian faith. And the revival has crossed racial and class boundaries sporadically at best. The Southern Baptist Convention was birthed in 1845, when Baptists in eight southern states, headed by Virginia, parted from northern Baptists who would no longer suffer brethren approving of slavery. By the 1870s, when the SBC voiced commitment to black evangelization but still would not allow blacks full membership, southern blacks began to launch their own denominations. Later outbursts of revivalism, such as the 1906–9 Azusa Street revival, would encompass blacks and whites and cross class lines (and include female as well as male clergy leadership), yet as descendants of Azusa Street revivalism climbed the social ladder, their churches adopted racial and class segregation.[7]

More profoundly, revivalism assumes an individualistic understanding of the human's basic constitution, as well as the human relation to God. It appeals to and aspires to revive something already latent in each individual, apart from any social relations or connections. Each separate soul is linked directly to God, as if by a spiritual chain of smoldering embers. What the ebbing, dying-but-not-entirely dead soul needs primarily is to have those independent links resuscitated, blown on by the Spirit and reignited into fiery life. The revivalistic *gathering* is simply instrumental, a vehicle where individuals as individuals reconnect with God. At an extreme, this individualistic reconnection can be ecstatic and clearly cut off from other people: in 1801, at Cane Ridge, Kentucky, people fell into solipsistic fits of laughter and barked up trees. In these spectacular raptures, each soul may have communed with God but hardly communicated with one another. Less dramatically but no less individualistically, solitary souls walked the sawdust trail alone or did not walk it at all. Later customs would emphasize the immediate connection to God, unaccompanied by others in the congregation, when revivalists would call for "every eye closed, every head bowed," and ask only those beckoned by God to raise their hands and be called to the altar for a confession of faith. In the border south of the Oklahoma Panhandle, I grew up with periodic revivals at which we robustly sang "I come to the garden *alone*," to stroll with Jesus as sole companion. Even more bluntly, our youth group rang out choruses of "Me and Jesus got our own thing going."[8]

Revivalistic Christianity makes social gatherings secondary and instrumental in the sense that it presumes this already existing individual relation of each to his or her own God, and fosters a spirituality that sees the most basic relation to God realized not in corporate gathering but in individual devotion. After their revival, the revived scatter to their isolated homesteads and pray and read the Bible for themselves. (In some areas, such as the mountainous Appalachians, local churches were served by circuit-riding preachers and gathered as a whole only once a month.) Conceptions such as the Southern Baptist "soul competency" emphasize the ability of each individual soul to be responsible for its relation to God, apart from interfering priests and the support of the social body as a whole. Gathered or corporate worship is an occasion to "recharge [individual] batteries," not an occasion to recognize and celebrate how each is more fully himself or herself only in relation to one another and as a social body in relation to God. With such a disposition, it is no surprise that revivalistic Christianity, even more than Protestantism in general, has in the face of disagreement all too freely resorted to schism, to the creation of new Christian denominations.[9]

Revivalistic democracy is wary of differences and heavy on moral prescription—you may belong with us when and if you behave and believe as we do. At times these moral prescriptions can lose any clear connection with the Christ of the Gospels and Christian tradition. So in the revivalism of my upbringing, the marks of genuine Christianity were teetotaling, refraining from cussing, and not smoking. This though Jesus drank wine, worried about many things more than "strong language" (the swearing or "oaths" the Gospels explicitly forbid would relate less directly to bawdy or earthy talk than to reciting the pledge of allegiance or promising absolute veracity on a Bible for testimony in a courtroom), and of course knew nothing of tobacco one way or the other. In such a routinized revivalism, people are reconciled not so much to the God of the Bible and Christian history as they are bound to social conventions considered at least vaguely Christian. As H. Richard Niebuhr puts it in his overview of American revivalism, "Men were now saved not from the frustration, conflict, futility and poverty of life which they sought to escape in the saloons; they were saved from whisky."[10] Of course, such conventionalized revivalistic democracy is not necessarily explicitly religious. It can be and has been secularized. Revivalistic democracy lays emphasis on negative freedom, freedom *from* direction or interference by any corporate, social reality—even the discerning congregation, but especially from "priests" or any others whose authority is derived historically and from beyond the locality.[11]

True to its emphasis on already existing, if dormant or latent, tendencies, revivalistic democracy also inclines to stress a bygone golden age. The revivalistic democracy yearns to return to its supposedly more perfect, harmonious past. In religious terms, it must once again revive itself as a Christian nation. In secular terms, it needs to regain a dominant ethnicity or guard the primacy of English as the only American language, or otherwise renew in the present a simpler, clearer history now perilously forgotten or at least overshadowed. It will in all events not rest easily with the notion of bringing into the democracy those races or languages or behaviors presumably not included in the golden age.

Democracy as parade and democracy as revival are not entirely at odds, nor is revivalistic democracy without its salutary aspects. Though I think the democratic parade offers important corrections to revivalistic democracy, southern, revivalistic democracy insists more clearly on a role for the Christian church in America's history and its present. Open to a wide variety of difference, the democratic parade can, like a ship loaded in ignorance of its actual construction, yaw too severely and precipitously toward thoroughgoing secularism. Though the United States has not been and ought not to become a "Christian nation," the predominance of Christian citizenry past and present, as well as the inherently public (and not merely private) nature of historic Christianity, means that this faith—along with others—must be given its due in the unfolding of the American identity. Revivalistic democracy has a point when it argues that religion has a place in the public square and should not simply be left at home. When the prophet Amos prayed, "Let justice roll down like waters" (Amos 5:24), he was not merely hoping for a flood in his prayer closet.

ᚦᚦᚦᚦᚦᚦᚦ

But how is it, in more immediate terms, that revivalistic democracy and other aspects of southern identity have—nearly 150 years after the Civil War—come to be so dominant in the entire nation's identity? In the 1960s and early 1970s the South and its conservatism were not nationally powerful, and certainly not seen as the vanguard of the country's future. Even now, some commentators wonder how national attitudes and policies are supported by vast swaths of the electorate across the "heartland," especially when many of these policies run against the economic interests of rural and working-class citizens in general.[12] We can draw a sharper bead on the rebirth of the South and the remaking of the nation in its image by some attention to the political phenomenon that is now routinely referred to as the Southern Strategy.[13]

The Southern Strategy and its success makes sense against the backdrop of the South coming into its own in the second half of the twentieth century. Historian Bertram Wyatt-Brown observes, "In matters of economic prosperity, racial demography, urbanization, and politics, the fact is that the [South] has altered much more since the early 1940s than it changed between 1865 and 1941."[14] Famously, the superiority of the North in population and industrial production played key roles in the South's Civil War defeat. Sparsely inhabited, industrially narrow and underdeveloped, and scarred by the wounds slavery inflicted on the oppressed and oppressors, the South "remained more or less fully in the frontier stage" for much of its antebellum history.[15] After the war, the humiliating and tumultuous periods of Reconstruction (perceived as hateful occupation by the "Yankee aggressors") and post-Reconstruction left the region preoccupied with the past, running in survival mode through the early decades of the twentieth century. The ennui and decline dipped to its nadir during the Great Depression. It is a mark of the desperation of the region that, despite its innate anti-government attitudes, the South saw Franklin Delano Roosevelt with his massive New Deal initiative as a savior. As a North Carolina textile worker commented, "Roosevelt is the only president we ever had that thought the Constitution belonged to the poor man too."[16] FDR would secure overall southern loyalty to the Democratic Party for four more decades, and the public works programs he instituted would begin to lift many southern noses above the lapping waters of poverty that had constantly threatened drowning.

Other factors came into play as the South sharply ascended after World War II. Cheap labor and low costs of living drew industry and economic growth. The advent of central air conditioning made sweltering southern summers palatable to those who otherwise resisted moving to the region. As northern and upper midwestern states started suffering economic erosion and the unappealing label of the Rust Belt, the South burst through clouds and shone as the Sun Belt. In the last few decades of the twentieth century, Southern demographics soared. From 1970 to 1990, the population of the eleven states of the Confederacy,[17] with Kentucky, grew by 40 percent—twice the national growth rate.[18] This not only increased the South's economic power and presence; it shifted electoral apportionments and increased southern political power as well. By the mid-1990s, the eleven states of the Confederacy, along with Kentucky and Oklahoma, added members in the House of Representatives, while northern states such as New York and Massachusetts dwindled in representation.[19]

The political architects of the Southern Strategy were well aware of these population shifts. More, they were southerners themselves and intuited an ongoing sense of disgruntlement with the federal government and northeastern elites. The seeding of the Southern Strategy may be dated to the 1948 Democratic National Convention. Even as the Democratic Party would continue for decades its dominance in the South, southerners nurtured memories of the Civil War as a great lost cause, and clung to a sense of the South as the essence of American identity and hopes. At the 1948 convention, President Harry Truman sympathized with civil rights, and Minnesota Senator Hubert Humphrey successfully urged platform planks that would provide federal protection against lynching, eliminate poll taxes, and set up national agencies to inhibit racist hiring practices. South Carolina Governor Strom Thurmond was among the southern Democrats who perceived these initiatives as federal meddling, scratching the scabs off ever-fresh memories of Reconstruction and other interference from Washington. Thurmond steamed out of the Philadelphia convention in revulsion. Months later, he assembled with 6,000 other southern Democrats in Birmingham and was nominated the presidential candidate of the newly formed States' Rights Democratic Party (soon enough dubbed the "Dixiecrats"). In the national elections, the Dixiecrats carried only Alabama, Louisiana, Mississippi, and South Carolina. The Dixiecrats died as a party but revealed an itch that would welcome a lot more scratching. Thurmond was elected—as a write-in candidate, the first in national history—to the U.S. Senate in 1954. He would fight against federal desegregation of the schools and the Civil Rights Act of 1957 and continue his long career well beyond the 1950s.

A young man named Harry Dent was an aide to Senator Thurmond. Bright and absorbent, Dent watched and learned, and by 1968 he worked on Richard Nixon's presidential campaign staff. The year 1968 might well be the year best recognized as the birthdate of the Southern Strategy. Nixon needed a healthy portion of the southern vote to win. His staff feared an erosion of ballots siphoning off to independent presidential candidate George Wallace. The Alabama governor campaigned with a banner slogan that, ironically, would later be adopted by abortion-rights advocates of the Democratic Party: "freedom of choice." Wallace was rough-edged and obviously tapped into racist sentiments. (Also, Wallace with his "Country and Western Marxism" was wary of big business as well as big government, a problem for any candidacy seriously desiring the Republican Party nomination.)[20] It was the unsavory genius of Dent and his successors to devise only apparently nonracist means to appeal to a rapidly coagulating and solidifying congeries of angry white southerners. These southerners—and soon enough other Americans in their wake—wanted Washington off their back and were sick of bleeding-heart-liberal social policies, often implemented by Ivy League intellectuals. Following Dent's game plan, Nixon and the Republicans won the South. Dent poked a big hole in the Democratic dam that had formerly secured an ocean of southern votes. The dike would erode quickly and crumble altogether by the 1980s, when Republicans secured both the presidency and control of the House of Representatives. Consider not only that four of the six presidents since Nixon have been Republicans, but that the two Democrats elected to the highest office hailed from Georgia and Arkansas. Not only have the Democrats been unable to place in power a presidential candidate who wasn't a southerner—the northeastern Democratic candidates have found their base in Massachusetts effectively used against them to deter votes in the South, West, and heartland.

After Dent, the Southern Strategy was honed by Lee Atwater. As a political novitiate, Atwater interned for Thurmond and was eventually mentored by Dent. Atwater matured as an operative by running Ronald Reagan's South Carolina presidential campaign in 1980 and subsequently helmed George H. W. Bush's 1988 national campaign. It was then that Atwater created the famous Willie Horton television ad, picturing a black convict who was paroled from a Massachusetts prison and later rearrested for a new crime of murder. Since Horton was paroled during the watch of Massachusetts Governor Michael Dukakis, the Democratic candidate for president, Atwater could use Horton's mugshot to play on race and class fears. The racism and classism were not all that subtle, yet were veiled. Over the years, leaders of the Southern Strategy had developed a series of code words that worked along similar lines. "Law and order" was not blatantly racist, but it connected with amorphous suburban and heartland anxieties about restless urban black masses.[21] "Welfare queen" suggested that welfare was a fraudulent system pandering to the indolent, deservedly poor same masses. "Affirmative action" was reframed as "reverse discrimination." And so on.

The Southern Strategy has proven so successful that it and variants on it have become conventional wisdom in national politics. George

W. Bush's political mastermind, Karl Rove, a college friend of Lee Atwater, extended the wedge tactics of fear and resentment with potent exploitation of the country's roiled post-9/11 psyche. The nationalization of politics via means of the Southern Strategy epitomizes in the virulent culture wars and, most precisely, the polarized categorization of red states vs. blue states.

༺༺༺༺༺༺༺

With its wedge tactics and exploitation of racism and resentment, the Southern Strategy is a politics of negativity. Its nationalization accounts for much of the polarization, small-mindedness, and ugliness of electoral politics as we currently know them. But it would be a mistake to think that the southernization of America is explained only by the Southern Strategy, or that the nation's southernization as a whole is generally as divisive and destructive as the Southern Strategy. The deeper and wider truth is that America's southernization signals the emergence of the importance of culture in national life, public as well as private. The Southern Strategy is a negative manipulation and expression of culture, but culture can be appealed to constructively as well as negatively. The Republican Party of recent decades has learned that economics and economic self-interest are not the only motivators of the citizenry. Citizens are also, and more fundamentally, motivated and energized by cultural identifications and commitments. Perhaps more than any other region of the country, the South has maintained vital culture and cultural identification. As the rest of the country catches up to the formative and transformative powers of culture, it is in this regard southernizing.

Culture, put directly, is what makes us human by a vast variety of particular ways and means.[22] Culture is a cultivating process that forms a certain kind of people and persons. Language, rituals, purpose-defining stories, and artistic creation are at the heart of culture. It is through such means—the means of culture—that we organize, categorize, and interpret our existence. Providing the means to understand ourselves and the purpose or goal of our existence and our endeavors, culture is that aspect of our existence undergirding all our thinking, feeling, imagining, and acting. To concretize this, we can reflect on how Americans come to be Americans by processes of enculturation. We learn not only a predominant literal language (English), but a strong figurative language. Concepts like "freedom" and "equality" are basic to this "language." The grammar of democracy and human rights, not that of monarchy and divine entitlement, is basic to the American language. We are taught this language not only directly, but through stories and rituals that rehearse it and provide its proper context. Schools teach us the stories of George Washington, Benjamin Franklin, Abraham Lincoln, W. E. B. DuBois, and other exemplars of what it means to be an American. Our calendars, the cultural organization of our time, are dotted with Thanksgiving, Independence Day, and other ritualistic rehearsals of the American identity. The creative arts give us literature, song, film, art, and other celebrations and encapsulations of Americanism. So it is culture, in many manifestations, that imparts to us our sense of the American "we," who we are and what we are about as a people.

In its most comprehensive forms, culture names people (grants them an identity) and infuses their lives with significance by providing an interpretation of their origins (where they came from) and their destiny (where they are going, their ultimate aim or goal).[23] Accordingly, it is clear why comprehensive cultures each have a sort of religion at their core. A religion encompasses the highest and most comprehensive ends of human identity and endeavor. So Christianity, for instance, holds that human beings exist first and foremost to praise and serve God. But a "religion" in this most general sense need not necessarily be theistic or name any God or gods. Marxism informs and forms people to believe and act as if human beings exist first and foremost to praise and serve posterity, to mutate, gradually and at times explosively, into a worldwide communistic proletariat. In recognition of these realities, the theologian Paul Tillich calls religion in general a matter of whatever is a people's "ultimate concern" and notes that such religion can take both sacred and secular forms. Where one's highest and most comprehensive allegiance lies—there is one's real worship.[24] As Tillich summarizes the matter, "Religion as ultimate concern is the meaning-giving substance of culture, and culture is the totality of forms in which the basic concern of religion expresses itself. In abbreviation: religion is the substance of culture, culture is the form of religion."[25]

In this light, we can see that culture is more basic than politics and economics. In fact, politics and economics are aspects of culture. While the Democratic Party has paid great attention to ringing the notes of economics and economic appeals to its constituency, it has been largely tone-deaf to the bass chords of culture that undergird economics. The South is that region of our country that has long been keenly aware and appreciative of culture, and how a specific, incarnate, comprehensive culture is more basic than any single aspect (economic, political, or otherwise) of culture, no matter how important that single aspect.

We can begin to get a grip on the profound southern appreciation of culture by turning to W. J. Cash (no known relation to Johnny), that acutely intuitive if somewhat florid analyst of *The Mind of the South.* Cash, himself a native southerner, points to several aspects of culture that could, in the Old South, help a southerner—commoner as well as plantation master—uphold a strong sense of identity and self-esteem. Displays of physical courage, a capacity for strong drink, the ability to gamble with steely resolve—all these and more cultural traits "are at least as important as possessions and infinitely more important than heraldic [ancestral] crests. In the South, if your neighbor overshadowed you in the number of his slaves, you could outshoot him or outfiddle him, and in your own eyes, and in those of many of your fellows, remain essentially as good a man as he."[26] Southern democratic and can-do frontier sensibilities, then, demanded an interest in a wide variety of cultural excellences or possibilities. It was not only the wealthy man or the prestigious senator who could be respected and admired. The conduct of honor, or musical abilities, or oratorical flourishes were cultural excellences more widely available and attainable than great wealth or political power. In the South, culture has long had a profound value for status and stature.

What's more, consider that throughout history, and even today in relatively democratic societies, the cultural pursuits of governmental politics and plutocracy (rule by wealth) have been accessible only to a small circle of men and (occasionally) women. Subalterns, those who possess little political or economic power, then naturally turn to other cultural practices of potency and influence. For the masses in the lower classes, especially when they are not politically organized, culture more broadly conceived was and is the only considerable power at hand. After the Civil War and well into the twentieth century, the South possessed lesser political and economic power than other regions of the country (certainly less so than the northeastern "establishment"). It is no accident that Southern literature came into its own in the first half of the twentieth century. Then, under the humiliating shadow of the Lost Cause, Wolfe, Faulkner, O'Connor, and others made vital contributions to the national culture. From an even more subjugated position, black southern Americans built on liberating spirituals and intricate African rhythms to brew jazz and the blues. And it was steeping in the blues pot that eventually gave the nation—and the world—country music, rock music, and soul music. American popular music simply is southern music. And there could be no southern music without black music. In government, popular music, and athletics, the southern influence is now predominant across the nation. Add to this the recognition that American popular culture now blankets most of the globe, bringing American attitudes and convictions to play (for good and ill) even more pervasively and effectively than massive American military might, and you behold another important respect in which the South did not ultimately lose the Civil War.[27]

❄❄❄❄❄❄❄

Later I will elaborate on how southern religion, particularly Christian evangelicalism and the African American church, has contributed to the southernization of America. For now, I underscore the importance of culture to the nation's destiny and the South's key role in building American culture as it stands. While we should never neglect the weight of political and economic power, it is culture that undergirds politics and economics. Culture creates the terms of consent or dissent by which the wider population engages the political and the economic. The discouraging face of this truth is that southern culture as it is now regnant is not altogether leading the nation in the direction in which it should go. The more encouraging face of the same truth is that culture is not a law of nature; as the preeminent expression of humanity, it is open to intervention and invention. It is dynamic and continually developing or unfolding. So revivalistic democracy need not be the final word in the American experiment. Happily, southern culture has its own resources for the appreciation and reinforcement of the democratic parade. In this regard, it might come alongside Yankees and other Americans who question the viability and attraction of democracy as revival.

Revivalistic democracy, as I see it, cripples itself and the country with its overweening inclinations to individualism, schismatic divisiveness, a yen for a nostalgically and falsely conceived past golden age, and anti-intellectualism. This democracy has all too easily played into the Southern Strategy (as well as the increased militarization of American identity). Democracy as parade, by contrast, is more socially minded, inclusive, and concerned to pursue goods commonly and widely held. Are there not only southern but theological grounds for curtailing democracy as revival and bolstering democracy as parade?

Sweetly, the theological and southern grounds for that bolstering come together in the person and work of Johnny Cash.[28] In 1969, at another time of bitter division in the United States, Richard Goldstein declared in *Vogue,* "It's hard to believe there's someone left around here who can plug me and the people of Nashville into the same socket. But if anyone can bring us together, it's Johnny Cash." In the same year, another northeastern critic said Cash "was bringing the country together with an authority that nobody else possesses in this fragmented nation. Johnny Cash knew how to talk to prisoners and presidents. He knew, as a matter of fact, how to talk to all of America."[29]

For decades, Cash's songs had admired and resonated with the American working people. In 1968, after years out of the limelight, he returned to national recognition with his recording at Folsom Prison. His songs salute "the ragged old flag" and America north and south, east to west. He was a premier country singer, an exemplar of the music beloved in what we now call the red states. His ABC television show included guests like blue-state favorites hippie Neil Young, folkie Joni Mitchell, and countercultural troubadour Bob

Dylan. In all, the democracy Cash embodied was democracy as parade, finding a common direction and hope for hippies and rednecks, convicts and preachers, lineworkers and corporate executives.

This democracy Cash saw both challenged and supported by a Christian gospel reluctant to condemn and cast out, but ready to offer grace and gather in. That gospel fittingly showed itself in a Tom Waits song Cash rendered in 1994. "Down There by the Train" taps into the longstanding country and gospel traditions of the train song.[30] Cash himself had reprised such country-train-song chestnuts as "The Wabash Cannonball" and "The Orange Blossom Special," and one of his earliest hits was his own "Hey Porter," with an ebullient southern rider on a train rolling back home to Dixie. Waits's song echoes the gospel-music figure of the train bound for heaven or the promised land (consider such classics as Sister Rosetta Tharpe's "The Gospel Train"). Likely to Cash's pleasure, Waits's train rattles by a station of apparent southern provenance, where the native flora include the willow and the dogwood.

Interestingly, this train doesn't stop at the station, but only "goes slow." Perhaps it is an ongoing, unending boxcarred parade, always available for boarding by anyone who makes it to the station. After all, you can hear this engine's whistle from "the halls of heaven to the gates of hell." For eternity's railroad schedule, arriving any time is "on time." Perhaps this train's promise is exactly its ability to move, to transport riders to another, better place, on a ride that can never begin too soon and so can never end or fully stop at any earthly destination. In all events, the train is open to every comer, and the lyrics emphasize that those who board must ride not by merit but by need— the passengers are "whores" and other shameful, forsaken souls. No one can buy a ticket to board this railroad. You must not be too proud to bum a ride, to slip onto the moving train like a penniless hobo. Passengers ride by grace, not by anything they have earned. And the gospel represented in this gospel song verges toward universalism, extolling a grace without limits. The train then is not the only parade in progress. There is also a ragtag procession of all types and kinds of needful people, making their way to the station swiftly or laboriously. The song's most striking lines suggest that the station-bound marchers come not only separately but in merciful aid to and with others: the narrator foreswears eye-for-an-eye vengefulness and sees Jusas Iscariot carrying John Wilkes Booth to the slowed train.

Judas Iscariot and Booth are both murderers of great men. Both are actors living out desperate "roles"—Booth quite obviously, as a thespian assassinating Abraham Lincoln in a theatre; Judas meeting Jesus' strange expectation that he would assume the role of the Messiah's betrayer (John 13:21–30). Both are dividers. Booth lashes out in hateful spite at the national union secured by Lincoln, while Judas is the first to break the bonds of Christ's variegated band of disciples. The pair are also alike ultimately as outcasts, with Booth hounded to his death in a burning Virginia barn and Judas hanging himself in a desolate field. Yet the compelling grace of the gospel train overcomes these treacherous traits. Even such arch sinners are not beyond redemption. And in a way their redemption has begun even before they reach the train, with Judas lifting the broken-legged Booth onto his back and the willful Booth letting himself be borne.

In remarking on this song, I of course do not mean to conflate American democracy (revivalistic or parade) with the church, or the American creed with the Apostles' Creed. Rather, let us imagine that the slow, rolling train is the kingdom of God, witnessed and pointed to by the gospel and the church's life under the gospel, but not contained or controlled by any earthly institution—not by the church and certainly not by the nation-state America. This train runs on rails not made by mortals, crossing all national borders. It is best recognized by those who see shared humanity most acutely in our mutual need, who look at the other not as a scapegoat or a demonic "other," but as a fellow sinner and potential copassenger.

Cash surely owned the character of the narrator of "Down There by the Train," a man capable of abandoning family and friends, one who has all too often "taken the low road." Because of the compelling train and its promise, this is exactly the man who can invite other low-road travelers to meet him at the station. I wonder if Kris Kristofferson had this song, with its evocation of the notorious presidential assassin, in the back of his mind when he eulogized Cash at his funeral as "Abraham Lincoln with a wild side."[31] Not all southerners would relish comparison with the Great Emancipator and dogged Preserver of the Union, but I suspect Johnny Cash would have approved.

Chapter 2

Lonesomeness and Community

Driving across the top of Indiana, I passed an SUV with a red, white, and blue bumper sticker bearing the legend "Freedom—Honor—Liberty." As any high school student of history knows, the United States has long esteemed freedom as one of its highest goods. And this has often, even usually, meant freedom as the absence of interference and impediment of others in an individual's pursuit of his or her goals and happiness. Yet the same student also knows there have been other significant American goods. Equality—as in "all men are created equal"—is one of them. What struck me about the bumper sticker was not only the absence of equality in this brief litany of American ideals, but the fact that freedom has become so important that it must be saluted twice, albeit with a synonym the second time.

Of course, the SUV itself speaks volumes about the premium we Americans put on individualism and independence. The SUV guzzles gas and provides a less comfortable and quiet ride than considerably cheaper sedans or midsized cars. SUVs are necessarily boxlike and lumbering, not at all streamlined like a sports car, and just a tad sexier than the buses they essentially are. In parking lots or other tight spaces they maneuver about as gracefully as a sumo wrestler in a suitcase. Even their vaunted safety has fallen into question, what with increased risk of rollovers. What alone commends them is their sheer size and powerfulness. The SUV driver sits as high as or higher than the drivers of most of the surrounding vehicles, master over all to be surveyed, and his or her three-ton chariot takes up the space and demands respectful notice like East Indian royalty towering atop their elephant-borne howdahs. The SUV, as various model names hint, connotes the unhindered getaway or trek away from customary ties and expectations (Escape, Expedition, Explorer), the responsibility-free, wide-open possibilities of the Wild West (Durango, Aspen, Sierra), the assured superiority of the fighter plane or battleship in need of no compelling name, just blunt letters and numbers (F-150). You can believe an American, especially an SUV-driving American, when his three-word bumper sticker tells you twice that he will not be tied down, bound, or limited.

And so we encounter a great American contradiction. As never before in our history, we prize individualistic liberty above all other goods, but we refuse to recognize that favoring this good so extremely may inhibit or even eliminate the realization of other goods. We want to be self-sufficient, yet loved and loving. We each want to do everything on our own terms, and yet simultaneously belong to a community. We desire our self-interested freedom from others above all things, and at the same time we want never to be lonely.

※※※※※※※

Lonesomeness is neither new nor unique to twenty-first-century Americans. Aristotle was right about many things, and one of them was his insistence that humans are social animals, desirous of companionship and lessened by its absence. What is unique to our time and place is the pervasiveness of loneliness in our society, coupled with our inability or refusal to admit we are lonely and to recognize ways in which our way of life promotes loneliness and hinders friendship and real (as opposed to virtual or mass-mediated) community. The vast majority of us now live in more densely populated areas than our ancestors. Yet we have less anchorage in communal commitments and celebrations than they had. And we are apparently more afraid of loneliness than they were. Our general aversion to silence is one indicator of our fear. With constantly droning televisions in homes, airports, and restaurants, and with iPods and other portable technological means, we never have to face a quietness that might divulge our solitude, either amid crowds of strangers or when we are temporarily and literally alone.

Emma Bell Miles, when she was nine, moved with her parents from Evansville, Indiana, to Walden's Ridge, near Chattanooga, Tennessee. There she was very much a part of the Appalachians, growing up among the quintessential "hillbillies." Her mother and father were educators and reared her as a cultivated woman, with skills in drawing, painting, and writing. She married young to a native hillbilly—against her parents' wishes—and spent the rest of her life largely in the remote forests and hills of Walden's Ridge. But Miles was a border-crosser. She had acquired skills of reflection and articulation anomalous among the hill folk, and often shuttled down to Chattanooga. There she lodged with wealthy and socially prominent friends. She attended orchestral concerts, painted murals in ornate drawing rooms, and wrote articles published in such esteemed magazine venues as *Harper's Monthly, Putnam's,* and *Lippincott's.* Her writings include the elegiac book *The Spirit of the Mountains* (originally published in 1905), surely one of our most precious and telling glimpses into the lives of "uncultured," rural Americans—hillbillies, indeed—who could not so effectively describe themselves and their ways to more urban and "modernized" Americans.[1] But this is by no means to say that Miles saw her friends and neighbors on the ridge as shallow people. On the contrary, in one of her typically penetrating and lyrical passages, she comments, "Solitude is deep water, and small boats do not ride well in it. Only a superficial observer could fail to understand that the mountain people really love their wilderness—love it for its beauty, for its freedom."[2]

Page after page of her vivid book testifies to the profound treasures of aloneness and quiet in a genuinely beautiful and untouched natural setting. There are no radios or televisions or roaring traffic, so that owls are heard hooting from deep in the surrounding wood. Hours pass with no sounds other than chickens pecking at seeds in the dirt outside the cabin door, and the click and clack of a mother working her loom to clothe her family. Vast sunsets, dawns blooming like flowers, the change of seasons evinced by color shifts in trees and grass, the gurgling clarity of unpolluted creeks and springs, the horizons beckoning breathtakingly from atop high places, and the shadowed harbors sheltering homes among the pines—Miles describes all of these with eloquence and the close attention of decades of observation and participation. "To all who understand these high solitudes it is no marvel that the inhabitants should be mystics, dreamers, given to fancies often absurd, but often wildly sweet." Some of course move away from the cabins and outhouses and comparative poverty, but many or most "cling to the ungracious acres they have patiently and hardly won, because of the wild world that lies outside their puny fences, because of the dream-vistas, blue and violet, that lead their eyes afar among the hills."[3]

In like vein, Miles recognized that the "luxuries" of the hill folk were "all romances," and included "music, whiskey, firelight, religion, and fighting." Chapter 8 of her book focuses on mountain music. The chapter appeared first as an essay in *Harper's*, and is still recognized as one of the most insightful early commentaries on the folk music that would soon come to be known as "hillbilly," then as "country and western," and finally as "country" music. Noting that her Appalachian neighbors had no theatres, bullfights, or sports arenas, Miles said of music that "it is their one emotional outlet." Commenting on the nasally, high-lonesome vocalization of the mountain singer, she remarked that "the oddly changing keys, the endings that leave the ear in expectation of something to follow, the quavers and falsettos, become in recurrence a haunting hint of the spirit-world; neither beneficent nor maleficent, neither devil nor angel—something not to be understood, yet to be certainly apprehended." Hillbillies, if I may respectfully resort to that term, did not theologize very explicitly, corralling spiritual realities or perceptions into systematized categories and giving them Latinate names. Nor did they complain, not in general, and certainly not about their lonesomeness in particular. But in their music they felt free to acknowledge loneliness and other pains, even to weep openly in the company of others. Loneliness is admitted and alleviated in church, where preaching and especially singing express grief and separation and long-felt agony in a way not otherwise noted in the stoic mountaineer's life.[4] Here is Miles at church, singing along and looking about:

> Tears are running down seamed and withered faces now, as the repression and loneliness of many months finds relief; the tune changes again, and yet again—they do not tire of this . . . [In these songs about meeting deceased fathers and mothers in heaven, the

singers anticipate] Broken ties restored, old pain of lonely nights to be no more—that is the dearest promise of this religion; the aching of old grief suddenly caught up and whirled away in this aroused hope of glory. 'By-and-by we'll go and see them . . .' Did ever Israel captive peer into the future any more wistfully than these?[5]

This break in loneliness, their rupture and rapture into communion both earthly and heavenly, is, says Miles, no small part of the church's deep attraction.

> I mean the break in loneliness of their lives, the meeting for once on a footing that is both decorous and friendly, of those who at almost any other time are isolated even more by peculiarity of temperament than by distance between their homes. What going to church really means to a woman who during the rest of the month sees hardly a face outside her family is difficult to realize.[6]

With these astute comments, Miles opens a doorway onto some of the deepest wellsprings of country music and its culture. The nose-singing, so easily ridiculed by those without an appreciation of it, is an art born of high altitudes that draw the breath upward, through chest and throat, converting the nasal passages into a reed instrument. It is an art born of overwhelming vistas that lift the face and spirit into the unfathomable, yet oh-so-blue-and-close heavens. The unguarded emotionalism of the singer and the music is not the typical expression of an uncouth rube who constantly lets fly with yips and yaws each and every ripple of feeling, but is the piercing sound of a pressure valve released only in song by an otherwise stoic and taciturn people. Likewise, the sometimes exaggerated, florid, pitiful, even self-mocking lyrics do not echo the early or organic country singer's everyday language offstage. Instead, the lyrics are the stunning, comparatively verbose and articulate statement of people who otherwise declare their preferences or hurt or yearnings monosyllabically, briefly, and bluntly, if at all.

ͷͷͷͷͷͷͷ

The culture of country music, then, has been a culture that admits loneliness and can name rather than deny its existence. A people who would face and embrace loneliness in song—even if it might overwhelm them and rip them apart no less viscerally than the wolves or panthers not so far from their cabin doors—took courage to welcome solitude and confess their dependence on powers greater than themselves. This explains how someone like Johnny Cash—tall, sturdily built, craggy-faced, and in possession of the most virile voice in the history of popular music—could cry out pitifully in song and never worry that his masculinity might be compromised. Cash's songs, like those of other country singers, are replete with complaints, wheedling, abjection, and weeping, entire litanies of misery and weakness induced by the vagaries of love, work, natural and humanmade disasters, God's silence, and so forth. In the performance of country songs, grown men and women can confess a dependence on mama so pathetic that it would be scorned in the (nonperformative) behavior of early teenage children. Country folk have prized their music so intensely because, as Miles sensed, it is the one medium in which they freely and openly confess their pain and need. Even today, after a few generations of therapeutic culture penetrating the entire nation, rural or rurally rooted folk esteem everyday stoicism and uncomplaining suffering. They prize country songs because they can identify with the singers, but moreso because the songwriters name and express hopes, desperations, disappointments, and vulnerabilities that are otherwise unnamed and unexpressed.[7]

No (male) country performer embodies this tense combination of everyday stoicism with unmitigated lament in song with more raw eloquence than the iconic Hank Williams. Growing up with an absent father, no stranger to poverty, dominated throughout his life by a willful mother, henpecked by wife Audrey, an alcoholic at least from his early teenage years, chronically afflicted by the excruciating pain of a congenital back condition, Hank had plentiful stock for lament and complaint. But in his conduct off the stage he displayed bravado, gun-toting aggressiveness, and insouciant disregard of his well-being and that of loved ones. Only in song did he vent his misery. And then, did he ever vent! On stage and on record he is utterly vulnerable, an open wound given larynx and language. His unmistakable singing is an outright bray, a succession of whines and blurts and sobs, not Whitman's bold "barbaric yawp" so much as a babe's wail of utter hunger and cold desperation.

Johnny Cash once told Bob Dylan that Williams's "I'm So Lonesome I Could Cry" was the saddest song he had ever heard.[8] Like other songs in Williams's repertoire, it is now an American standard, covered by jazz and rock and pop singers alike. The lyrics alone are powerful enough, but no rendition of the song makes it as vivid and expressive as Hank's own. His fluid braying and bawling, like much else in art, is partly invention born of necessity. In his earliest days, Williams performed without amplification: he had to sing brashly to be heard over guitars and fiddles. It is also, I suspect, a consequence of the stoic country culture that reserved unguarded emotional release and articulation for music.[9] The sole shield behind which the country singer summons courage to articulate his need is his guitar. Hank's stupendous load of misery was too big for his wiry, emaciated body. It had to come out somewhere, and in "I'm So Lonesome I Could Cry" the thorny bundle of agony seemed to be pulled directly up from his gut and out through his nose.[10]

So Hank's vocal performance makes his lyrics take on their own almost independent life. He is an intuitive and practiced master of onomatopoeia. A frequent resort to words beginning with or emphasizing the "m" sound ("midnight," "means," "moon," "time," and of course "lonesome") allows Hank to moan moaning lyrics. When he marks the sound of the "midnight train whinin' low," his "whinin'" is a literal whine, and the "low" that follows descends a fifth from the preceding word. In this endless night when "time goes crawlin' by," "crawlin'" crawls out of his mouth, extended into a two-word enunciation. When he thinks of his absent loved one and "wonder[s] where you are," "wonder" is also enunciated as two words—"*one*-der"—and transformed into a homonym for singleness and solitude. This yen for sound imitating the reality a word expresses is a central reason the steel guitar is a staple instrument in country music. The slide on strings allows the steel to itself whine, moan, laugh, mimic machine and animal sounds, startle in surprise, and so on. In this song, before Hank has dolefully sung a word, the steel anticipates with a plaintive, lilting cry quite like the forlorn train's whistle.

Another aspect of the song's performance demands mention. I have said that Williams's vocalization could be so primal and needy that it resembled an infant's inarticulate bawling. At times when Hank sings, his misery reduces him to the broken grammar of baby talk. In the closing lines of "Nobody's Lonesome for Me," he crumbles into a toddler who cannot speak a contraction, wailing that "nobody lonesome for me."[11] Similarly, in the third stanza of "I'm So Lonesome I Could Cry," Hank tells us the significance of the desolate robin mourning the onset of death "when the leaves begin to fall." He should say this "means" the robin is ready to give up, and earlier in the song he has used that word properly and fully. But this far into the lament he can summon only the strength and capacity of a two-year-old, and moan out "that *mean* he's lost the will to live."

With all this, we have not yet taken full notice of the song's sheer poetry.[12] Most popular songs (and, for that matter, most operatic arias) suffer when shorn of instrumentation and performance and exposed on the page as naked poems. "I'm So Lonesome I Could Cry" is an exception. Hank in fact originally wrote it to be recited, not sung, and worried that the song might sound too artsy to his rustic audiences. (Later he cited it as his personal favorite.)[13] It can serve as a textbook example of concise evocation of scene and mood, and of expansive anthropomorphization. The midnight train, the moon "hiding its face" behind clouds, a lone star falling "across a purple sky," the mournful whippoorwill and the fading robin—all these images simply and briefly convey a lonesomeness so vast that it overwhelms the entire landscape and even the cosmos.[14]

There was only one Hank Williams, and there is only one "I'm So Lonesome I Could Cry." But if few equal it poetically, many country songs walk right up to the abyss of loneliness and stare into its darkest depths. Country music's confrontation of the alienation inherent to the human condition can be nothing less than existential in scope. Unlike so much about our current national culture and politics, it admits the inevitability of suffering and the tragic, and acknowledges the creaturely limitations no mortal can escape.

⹋⹋⹋⹋⹋⹋⹋

The lonesomeness most freely confessed in country music is ostensibly that born of romantic pining or sexual lust. But country singers can be lonely for a variety of relationships or states of being. Country songs long for what was (a deceased mother, a happy home, a jilting lover) or what might be (reunion with mother after death, lakes filled with wine, the prisoner's freedom, escape from demeaning work and cruel bosses, the perfect and all-satisfying lover). The diversity of subjects, as well as the cosmic and existential sweep of romantic loneliness so strikingly portrayed by Hank, provide manifest clues that lonesomeness is a capacious and crucial category in country music.

Woody Guthrie told folklorist Alan Lomax that the blues (in all forms of music) is about lonesomeness. It may be lonesomeness for a lover, but alternatively lonesomeness for a job, for spending money, for good times, for estranged children, for getting out of jail. Guthrie thought the most searing blues traced back to the runaway slave, violently deprived of home and heritage, torn loose from family, fleeing for a freedom of vast uncertainty and insecurity. As Mark Zwonitzer and Charles Hirshberg note, commenting on the fugitive traveler in "Lonesome Road Blues," no destination may actually bring peace. "The terrifying discovery at the end of the road is that [the runaway's] got *no place* to be, no place except maybe the road itself. The best he can hope for is to get 'where the climate suits my clothes.' " This "terrifying discovery" that even the brightest hopes are suspended over nothingness, that even reaching an aim arduously desired may result only in new or renewed anxiety, is what makes the runaway slave "America's ultimate existential man."[15]

Of course, few country musicians are or have been African American, let alone runaway slaves. Yet country music is profoundly (if not often consciously) indebted to black music and the black American experience. The poor and working-class whites whence sprang early country music were impressed how well the blues encapsulated their own situations and anxieties—situations and anxieties that, when they stung or ached, were recognized as a kind of lonesomeness. Though not as severely deprived of rights or political and economic opportunities as were slaves, poor and working-class whites knew what it was to live in a world of dire limitations and constricted aspirations. Poor and underprivileged Americans, of whatever race, have often channeled their lonesomeness in two directions: into songs about sex and romantic love, and into songs about travel.

Sexual love is not a preoccupation confined to the lower classes. But it takes on special power when other opportunities of achievement and ecstasy are denied. When there is little or no hope for education or artistic pursuit, when holding political office is inconceivable, when work is soul-numbing drudgery with little dream of advancement, more weight rests on love and sex for the attainment of a life worthwhile and satisfying. Outside religion, successful and lasting love (or ongoing sexual prowess, with the ecstatic release and status it accrues) is the only resort for significance and joy. This explains why, in country and other popular musics, lost love is sung about so melodramatically. In many popular songs, the catastrophic effects of the failure of romantic love are exaggerated to a cosmic scale. In "Big River," Johnny Cash's jilted lover "taught the weeping willow how to cry" and made the "clouds cover up a clear blue sky"—his very tears will flood and wash away the big river.[16] In part, such grandiose declarations reflect the bragging, tall-tale tradition of Paul Bunyan using redwoods for toothpicks and Pecos Bill lassoing a tornado. Moreso, they betray how important romantic love is in the lives of ordinary folk who have no other avenues for success and happiness. When love departs, then stars fall from the sky and the sun goes black—the crushing effect seems nothing short of apocalyptic, world-ending.

Angela Davis points to another reason sexuality recurs so frequently and significantly in popular music. The blues took shape after emancipation and (failed) Reconstruction. In most day-to-day affairs, the economic and political status of former slaves had not changed. African Americans remained extremely poor and vulnerable. One thing had changed for them. For the first time in America, they could choose their spouses and sexual partners, and not have them arbitrarily removed by a slavemaster at the auction block. Since they were still effectively without the vote and the means to do more than scratch out a living, sexuality presented one realm in which African Americans "could exercise autonomy—and thus tangibly distinguish their contemporary status from the history of enslavement." Sexual love was thus not merely sexual love but "physical and spiritual evidence . . . of freedom."[17] So it is certainly true that the blues frequently celebrate sex (and lament its vicissitudes). In doing so, however, they are not merely hedonistic or simply sensual. Instead, the blues are an affirmation of liberty, a liberty too much and too often curtailed in other areas of culture and politics. Once again, the conditions faced by poor and working-class whites were not as severe as those known by former slaves, but these too were people of stifled opportunity and frustrated aspiration. The country tradition of honky-tonkin' grew up among people punching timecards, indebted to the company store for groceries and sundry goods, overseen by taskmasters for backbreakingly long workdays. Many lived for the liberatory release of Saturday night, for its drink, dance, romance, and the chance of getting lucky with a "honky-tonk angel."

But sex is not the only instantiation and celebration of freedom in the blues and country music. Travel is another. The slave forcibly confined to a few acres for a lifetime, now freed, can at least dream of travel. In blues culture, the traveling musician enjoyed high status as an exemplar of freedom, someone who escaped the boredom and chronic despair of substandard employment and found a way to earn a living without relying on whites. Who has broken the short and brutal chains of slavery more tangibly and emphatically than the troubadour who can move from place to place at will?[18] Likewise, the country musician embodies mobility and liberty, the liberty to escape a dead place or dead job or dead relationship, the ability to stretch toward the wild world outside their "puny fences." So country singers adore movement and transport, as in Hank's "Ramblin' Man," Merle Haggard's "White Line Fever," and Cash's "I've Been Everywhere." Historian Bill Malone in fact suggests that "rambler" or some variation on it has been the most popular name for country bands.[19]

Despite their fleeting joys, however, sexual love and travel never completely banish lonesomeness and its hurt. Love and travel are both overburdened by outsized expectations. Romance is unstable and impermanent. So country songs depict the unbearable pain of lost love. Or they portray frightening rage and violence in response to sexual betrayal. Some of our earliest Appalachian folk songs—such as "Ommie Wise" and "Knoxville Girl"—chillingly relate the murder of a loved one. In "T for Texas," Jimmie Rodgers vows to shoot two-timing Thelma, "just to see her jump and fall."[20] In "Delia's Gone,"

Cash's even scarier narrator ties his unfaithful lover to a chair and plugs her twice.

Likewise, and as we have already seen with the ultimate existential American (the runaway slave), travel is not finally and completely satisfying. Every new place eventually becomes an old place, replete with many of the old problems. Soon every town looks the same, and you feel as if you've seen everything. Listen closely, and Hank's ramblin' man is not altogether happy—his recurrent urge to leave is in fact a kind of birth defect. And Haggard's "White Line Fever" is, after all, an illness. So country music can and does celebrate such liberations as sexual love and travel, but only for a song or two. Then lonesomeness rears its head again. In all its breadth—sexual, financial, spiritual, homesick, cultural, political—lonesomeness in country music acknowledges that the world is out of joint, that it lacks wholeness and fullness. In this world, things simply aren't as they should be, and it will do little good to pretend otherwise. Country music can be appallingly sentimental, but at its best it is three chords and the truth.

⁂⁂⁂⁂⁂⁂⁂

Looked at theologically, lonesomeness is an effect of our creatureliness, misappropriated. We are not self-creating, freestanding gods. We are instead the creatures of a God who alone is "self-sufficient" and can live and love only in God's triune self. As creatures, we are necessarily dependent—dependent certainly on God, but also on one another (the parents who birth us, the friends who sustain us) and on the wider creation that provides air, food, water, and much beauty besides. When Creator, creatures, and creation are in harmony, we creatures remain dependent but not lonely. When we deny our creatureliness and try to cast off all limitations, we alienate ourselves. Put more plainly, we make ourselves lonesome.

We modern or postmodern Americans may be the most lonely people in history.[21] So much of our national mythology feeds an overwrought sense of individualism and self-sufficiency. Our ancestors fled from the tired, corrupt, worn-out European world and attempted to found the kingdom of God on earth on these (apparently) barren shores. The aim was to create a new world, freshly and from the ground up. The vastness of the continent meant that the frontier—and the hopes of ever more newness, ever more ability to start over—spread westward over centuries, inculcating individualistic frontier mentalities in generation after generation of Americans. In point of fact, however, Americans have never actually been as sheerly individualistic as the national mythology has it. It is significant that the Pilgrims landing at Plymouth Rock arrived on these shores as a community of families, intending to found a new "commonwealth." They never meant to go it alone as self-made men and women. As the historian Perry Miller summarizes Puritan views of the seventeenth century, these early Americans believed community was not "an aggregation of individuals" but "an organism functioning for a definite purpose, with all parts subordinate to the whole."[22] (This communal and bodily language echoes the apostle Paul's in 1 Corinthians 12.) Well into the eighteenth century, Americans believed, as Presbyterian pastor Gilbert Tennent put it, that "we were born not merely for ourselves, but the Publick Good!"[23] Certainly frontier life demanded a degree of resourcefulness not necessary in urban settings, where a family did not have to produce its own clothes, candles, and crops. But even there, westward expansion occurred in mass only after government initiatives beginning under Jefferson explored and mapped the country; after government armies cleared land of its original, Indian owners; after government coordinated and subsidized the construction and operation of transcontinental railroads. Nineteenth-century mountain men—hunters and trappers—were perhaps the closest thing to the myth of the self-made, utterly self-reliant American. Yet they learned their trade from and sometimes lived with Native Americans. All this and more is obscured by our mythology of individualism. This mythology, certainly at its extremes, is nothing less than a denial of human creatureliness and creaturely interdependence.

In fact, individualism is expensive. Only the affluent can afford to live without a network of family, friends, neighbors, faith community, and government that will support them when sick and old; serve as a safety net through economic hard times; provide child care; build and maintain an infrastructure of sanitation, transportation, and communication; shelter and connect the newly arrived; and so on. In our day, only the affluent can readily afford the technologies that enable and facilitate relative isolation and denial of interpendence. Give each of us as an individual enough riches and tools, and we will be fine (if lonely) all on our own.[24] Accordingly, when affluent Americans find ourselves strangers to and threatened by our neighbors, we do not imagine how we might structure our lives and cities differently, so that our neighbors might no longer be strangers. Instead, we turn to the technological fix of bigger and better burglar alarms and electronic security systems.

Years ago, I spent a week or two in Cairo, Egypt. One evening, I sat outside, sipping tea on our host's veranda, overlooking the bustling streets of the city. As dusk descended, I noticed that our host was continually glancing ahead and down the sidewalk. Asked why, he replied that neighbors on the next block had a daughter attending evening classes. As she walked home alone, the neighbors saw her safely to her door under a chain of watching eyes, eyes belonging to cooks at their kitchen window, smokers on the stoop, hosts and guests relaxing on verandas. If at any point she did not make a timely appearance in front of a home on her route, that homeowner would straightaway investigate. Of course there was never any need—the friendly watching itself prevented any wrongdoers. Safety is one of the benefits of genuine neighborliness. By contrast, we Americans, certainly also concerned for the security of our sons and daughters, would buy the girl a cell phone. Here as in other ways, our response to the increasing threat of strangeness in our cities and neighborhoods is not to build more sidewalks, intermix residential and commercial zones, and otherwise imagine how we might recreate real neighborhoods. Instead, we look for the technological fix, which will, after all, preserve maximum individual independence.

Affluence and technology help to further explain the riddle mentioned in chapter 1—why is it that middle- and working-class Americans bought into the highly individualistic politics of the right, even as recent Republican policies so blatantly favor the extremely wealthy over the middle and lower classes? I noted in chapter 1 that it has been the Republican Right that has most astutely recognized the importance and power of culture in the American South and heartland. Many ordinary Americans sense that the erosion of community seriously rends the nation's fabric. They suspect not all that ails us as a people can be cured technologically or economically. However inadequately, then, the right has named a spiritual and cultural uneasiness that Democrats and the left have been slow even to acknowledge.

But exactly here we should note a significant wrinkle. Though the New Right named the working man's cultural uneasiness (as with worries about "traditional values"), the New Right did not originate among the working classes. As the historian Lisa McGirr shows, it first took root in the quite affluent enclave of Orange County, California. Journalists in the 1960s noted that Orange County was the center of America's conservative movement. Southern California's growth was fueled in no small part by the explosion of the defense industry during the Cold War. From 1945 to 1965, 62 percent of the national budget went to defense. Defense money drove development, especially in the Sunbelt South and the West, "and the biggest beneficiary was southern California."[25] In southern California, and centered in Orange County, there arose a vast array of construction: food, retail, service industries; churches and other centers of worship; and eventually tourism (think Disneyland). The governmentally funded defense industry attracted white-collar, educated workers who usually embraced right-wing politics. The rapid growth of building, food, service, and other support industries drew entrepreneurs, and libertarianism was popular in their business circles. Labor organization was steadfastly resisted. Accordingly, Orange County was, as McGirr puts it, "not tempered by liberal Jewish Democrats, organized workers, and vocal minorities." Like other conservative strongholds to follow in affluent regions of Texas, Arizona, Georgia, Louisiana, and Colorado, Orange County consisted mainly of a "socially homogenous group of highly skilled, affluent inhabitants and, often, the powerful presence of defense and military."[26] In this setting arose support for Barry Goldwater's 1964 presidential candidacy and, later and more successfully, Ronald Reagan's ascent to political prominence. For these early upper- and upper-middle-class backers of Goldwater, Reagan, and their successors, "Western libertarianism, combined with a theoretically incompatible social and cultural conservatism, came to make 'common sense.' "[27]

In short, though today's American right routinely abjures government, it has its origins in an affluent region profoundly indebted to works of government. Uncle Sam in mid-nineteenth century annexed what is now southern California from Mexican ranchers, later provided funds for an infrastructure of dams and irrigation systems (not to mention highways and the interstate system), infused magnificent sums into the region's burgeoning defense industry, and provided FHA loans for new housing. McGirr does not overstate with her observation that "Nowhere in the nation was the federal government more directly responsible for economic growth than in the building of the West."[28] But as she also notes, familiarity can breed contempt. Throughout the West in general, and in southern California in particular, the government's presence was pervasive. And it could be perceived as interfering, not least by business owners drawing on federal funds and hacking away firsthand at proliferating coils of bureaucratic red tape. The frontier-fed myth of individualism supplied an underlying, if illusory, insistence that Americans (especially western Americans) single-handedly made their own fortunes and destinies. This individualism occluded recognition of actual interdependence, with governmental and other supports. The affluent who had benefited most successfully from Uncle Sam's infrastructure and largesse now wanted government off their back. Orange County was the hothouse where the conservative renaissance took root and flowered; it then was subsequently seeded in other affluent regions such as Atlanta and Colorado Springs. A libertarian conservatism, it was not altogether in sync with the cultural, organic conservatism of the larger South and the heartlands. That grassroots, more populist and working-class conservatism resisted big business hardly less than big government. But the Orange County brand of conservatism not only spread to other affluent enclaves in the South and larger West. It there tapped into the typically promilitary attitudes of the less affluent citizens in those regions, and responded to the power of culture and religion among the same.

In sum, the New Right has accurately sensed the rising loneliness and breakdown of community and tradition afflicting Americans, and noticed acutely among working-class and middle-class citizens. Yet the New Right's origins and most powerful base lie not within these classes but among the much narrower strata of wealthiest Americans. These wealthiest Americans optimally possess the resources of affluence and technology to maintain security and comfort even as local and national community disintegrates.[29] The rich can afford lonesomeness. The rich, at least longer than the less wealthy and the poor, can survive without cultural, communal, and governmental support. The radically antigovernment ideology of the New Right has also provided cover for the richest Americans—its popular rhetoric helps occlude the degree to which current wealth was historically dependent for its generation on government support and subsidy.

From Reagan to George W. Bush, the New Right has attracted Americans across the economic spectrum by marrying "lower-taxes" libertarianism (especially advantageous to the most wealthy) to social conservatism (resonant with middle- and lower-class Americans worried about cultural and communal degradation). In political and cultural terms, it has been an extraordinarily successful marriage. However, perhaps partly because of its success, the New Right has gone to extremes that now threaten the marriage[30] and clearly have not served living democratic community, and indeed, real community of any other sort.

The nation is as sharply divided regionally as it has been at any time since the Civil War. This is due to wedge politics that majors on showing Americans how they desperately differ from one another. It is also due to a gap between the rich and the poor now at its widest since the Gilded Age (though not acknowledged in wedge politics) and plutocratic governance reaching its most brazen heights under Bush the junior and a compliant, special-interests-compromised legislative branch. It is due to an executive branch of government concentrating increased power and loathsome of the checks and balances of representative democracy. It is due to the weakening-unto-death of labor unions and other means that lent workers a viable voice. The nation's division is due to economic practices and attitudes that encourage people to look out only for themselves and to be as mobile and rootless as possible, to an overweening individualism that blinds us to our necessary ties with others and eschews any common good. All these developments cripple democracy and tear at communal ties, national and local. They leave us desperately lonesome without the wherewithal to so much as properly name and identify the causes of our lonesomeness, let alone work to alleviate it.

ᔑᔑᔑᔑᔑᔑ

As grim and contentious as the situation stands—as attenuated as American democracy now is—the nation is not without resources to alter its current, disastrous path. Forays toward a more robust democracy are suggested among the very southern, country-music loving, and largely Christian cultures we have been examining. Viewed through Christian lenses, as we have noted, individualism is illusory. Creatures are dependent and interdependent. Technologically enamored, plutocratic proponents of nationhood like to envision America as an invulnerable, innocent behemoth, able to overcome any and all limitations. Ronald Reagan represented this bizarrely inflated, wildly optimistic Americanism with his 1987 comment that, "The calendar can't measure America because we are meant to be an endless experiment in freedom, with no limit to our reaches, no boundaries to what we can do, no end point to our hopes."[31] This blatantly theological statement denies creatureliness and casts America in godlike terms. It makes the nation an entity without limits, infinite in power and reach, eternal in its endurance. Such attitudes have real-world consequences. They lie behind American attempts to control political affairs in societies across the globe, as well as a willful eagerness to dismiss the ecological damages and costs of our extravagantly consumeristic way of life. They imagine there will always be another technological fix, that the powerful and wealthy, at least, will be able to take care of themselves, and that human progress will continue indefinitely, if not forever. All these are strange, incongruous attitudes for what fashions itself as "conservatism." They are also rather infantile attitudes—the expectation of the infant that all else exists to serve its needs, that any limits set before it are only to be overcome by protest and ingenuity, that frustration is never to be endured but always removed by eliminating its sources. Such attitudes form citizens fit to live in a democracy for moral infants and adolescents, rather than a democracy for grown-ups.

Christians schooled in an Augustinian recognition of human realities can contribute much to a democracy for grown-ups. A democracy informed by Augustine's enduring insights would demand a
sober recognition of creatureliness and its limits. Though it would not
idealize suffering or countenance needless suffering, it would admit
that some suffering comes to all creatures. Creatures are not gods. We
are contingent beings. We live in a world and history much, much bigger than ourselves individually or corporately, exceeding the control
of any of our grandest designs. In a finite and limited world, we sometimes have to go without desired goods. There is an inescapably tragic
dimension to creaturely human life, in the sense that not all goods can
be pursued at once or in a single lifetime. For example, both marriage
and holy celibacy are goods. The goodness of marriage does not make
the monk's or nun's dedicated celibacy an evil, or vice versa. Marriage and committed celibacy are simply different goods. And no one
person can embody and live out both. One or the other good has to be
chosen, and the other relinquished. Such are the (small or great, mild
or severe) tragic dimensions of creaturely life. Here and in many other
ways—in terms of occupations, artistic pursuits, marriage partners,
and so on—our creatureliness means that we will know the pain of
choosing between two or more genuine goods, and letting go of the
good we subsequently must abandon.

Tragedy takes on a darker hue when sin and brokenness enter the picture. The realities of a world marred by sin and brokenness sometimes
necessitate the embrace of a "lesser evil" (divorce rather than abusive
marriage, and the horrible vagaries of a just war, might be two examples). But here we need only note that even ordinary, everyday life, without drama or crises, sounds tragic notes for creatures, simply because
we are finite, limited, dependent beings. And it is oftentimes the attempt
to deny such limits that exacerbates and worsens tragedies—as in the
case of the financier who can't be satisfied with more than enough *and*
cuts corners to enlarge her company even further, or the policeman who
wants to work with integrity *and* use illicit means to secure conviction
of a suspect. Most prosaically, we refer to our daily denial of the tragic
as the wish (the expectation?) to have our cake and eat it too. It's not difficult to enumerate instances of the great American tendency to ignore
our creatureliness and pretend we can live without any taste of the tragic:

The demand for government programs that benefit us or our neighbor-hood, alongside the insistent urge to pay fewer and fewer taxes; "lite," "lowfat," and other diet foods that promise all the pleasure of taste and consumption, but with no weight gain or clogged arteries; the privilege to drive gas-guzzling vehicles, alongside the entitled sense that gasoline must be cheap; a cure-obsessed medicine that seeks ever to push back death, alongside its refusal to help us face the death that remains finally inevitable for all of us.

Admitting our creatureliness means acknowledging that the tragic, in greater and lesser degree, in mundane and in more catastrophic cir-cumstances, is a fact of life. It is a recognition of traditional Chris-tianity, but it is not meaningful or sensible only to Christians. It inculcates and undergirds a set of virtues that marked many Ameri-cans well through World War II, and which has declined precipitously only with the post–World War II explosion of consumer capitalism. These are the virtues of what we might call democracy for grown-ups. Democracy is less dependent on hierarchical authority than other forms of government. It is government not simply *for* the people, but *by* the people. As such, it entails a high degree of self-government. To work, then, it demands a citizenry ready and able to assume the responsibilities of maturity. The virtues required of mature democrats have been esteemed by working-class and middle-class Americans, strongly exemplified in the South, the Midwest, and Southwest. They have been extolled by commentators on the "Okie culture" of the Dust Bowl migration, and in the "proprietary democracy" lauded by social critic Christopher Lasch.[32] They are also attitudes and disposi-tions often storied and admired in classic country music. Here are six cardinal virtues of democracy for grown-ups.

1. The virtue of hard work. Mature democrats respect manual labor and other forms of hard work, of truly *earning* a liv-ing. Their virtues jibe more with producer-oriented than consumer-oriented capitalism. A democracy of and for grown-ups honors straightforward, honest toil more than wealth accumulation through shrewdness, dealmaking, and luck.
2. The virtue of productive work and citizenship. Mature dem-ocrats are first and foremost productive citizens, not con-

sumers. They mean to do their part for the common good, seeing to their families and to the wider community. They desire meaningful political participation, giving them a voice in combating the overweening influences of leviathan government and monopolistic corporations.

3. The virtue of plain living and "simple pleasures." Ostentatious consumption is viewed as little less than moral weakness. Wastefulness is abhorred. It is good to live moderately, not put on airs, not worry much about "keeping up with the Joneses." Enough is enough, and can be enjoyed and celebrated as such.

4. The virtue of honor and integrity. Mature democrats do not seek stature via wealth or power so much as they prize being rightly and accurately known as honorable, trustworthy, and loyal.

5. The virtue of fortitude and survival with dignity. Citizens of a democracy for grown-ups do not expect life to be easy. It is in fact often a struggle. They hope and will work for alleviation of injustices and poverty, but they know human life will always be bounded by limits and met with unavoidable tragedy. They strive not to die "with the most toys" but to survive and eventually meet death with dignity.

6. The virtue of democracy itself. Mature democrats esteem democracy because it recognizes, however imperfectly, the transcendent equality of all people. They are not interested in airs, pretense, and empty spectacle. They also appreciate democracy because it limits the power of any one person, class, or institution. They have learned again and again through history that even the wisest and kindliest rulers have their blind spots and can be corrupted.

This set of virtues has been represented in the American character and still can elicit admiration and aspiration. These also are virtues that fit us to admit rather than deny tragedy in our lives. They aid maturation in a sometimes hard and always limited existence. These virtues can undergird and energize the recovery of democracy for grown-ups.

A democracy for grown-ups does not infantilize and pander to the less admirable angels of the American character. It recognizes that there is no eating the cake and having it too. It does not automatically turn politicians into liars by refusing ever to elect a candidate who honestly says some taxes must be raised. It looks not only to the well-being of oneself and one's nuclear family, but takes appropriate responsibility for the wider commonweal. It looks to posterity, realizing that many great goods cannot be realized in a single lifetime, but may with persistence over generations someday be enjoyed by those who come after us. Admitting limits and tragedy, it faces into and shoulders unavoidable suffering, rather than impatiently fleeing all discomfort or pain. In acknowledging our creatureliness and limits, it recognizes, with Martin Luther King Jr., that we are dependent on others for our survival and any prosperity we enjoy. As King said:

> Whether we realize it or not, each of us lives eternally "in the red." We are everlasting debtors to known and unknown men and women. When we arise in the morning, we go into the bathroom where we reach for a sponge which is provided for us by a Pacific islander. We reach for soap that is created for us by a European. Then at the table we drink coffee which is provided for us by a South American, or tea by a Chinese or cocoa by a west African. Before we leave for our jobs we are already beholden to half the world.[33]

King's remarks suggest that our creatureliness and creaturely limitations are not merely tragic but can be celebrated. Our dependence on others connects and ties us to them. In a rich sense, our dependence and common welfare are finally not so much tragic as comic. The Christian tradition ultimately affirms all will be well, that history will come out right in the end. But this can and will occur not through human effort. It is God alone who can bring God's kingdom to its fullness on earth. Sometimes God works through creaturely limitations and foibles; at other times God works in spite of them, bringing about unsuspected and unintended ends to our meddling means. The comic sensibility bred by awareness of these realities keeps us mortals from taking our projects too seriously. It wards off the despair so apt to follow the failure or less-than-total success of our mortal attempts to improve worldly conditions. At the same time, the comic sensibility resists easy capitulation to the status quo. It looks to the kingdom come and coming—a comic ending to the world's story—and challenges what is, on behalf of what might be.

The comic sensibility keeps us alert to irony and to our foibles as well as those of our leaders.

A democracy for grown-ups can also draw on the heritage of King and the African American church to embrace life as shot through with the comic as well as the tragic, as "both a carnival to enjoy and a battlefield on which to fight." As Cornel West observes, this hard-won heritage of a people surviving over centuries of oppression is marked by "engaged gaiety, subversive joy, and revolutionary patience which works for and looks for the kingdom to come. It is comic in that it breeds a defiant dissatisfaction with the present and encourages action. It is tragic in that it tempers exorbitant expectations."[34]

<hr />

Mention of America's extraordinary (and southern-based) black church tradition suggests new resonances for what I earlier explored under the rubric of democracy as parade. Martin Luther King and his followers took up the parade as a means of battle. They literally marched for justice and in their brave parades elicited responses that exposed the arbitrariness, hate, and blindness underlying their oppression. Parades, then, can challenge as well as celebrate. They make public grievances that the powerful hope to keep hidden and veiled as private. They exercise strength in numbers and especially in unity. And at their best and most challenging, they require grown-ups—people who will march with courage and persistence, in the face of potential and sometimes actual violence.

Revivalistic democracy, by contrast, is less amenable to a democracy for grown-ups. The revival concentrates on the individual and keeps faith, hope, and anger private. It is not so much progressive as regressive, calling people not forward so much as backward, to a supposed golden age, the immaculate warmth and safety of the womb. It emphasizes being born again (and again), continually starting over, and accordingly neglects the necessity and cultivation of maturation, of growing up.

Democracy for grown-ups, as parade, is of course not always

exemplified in country music. Plenty of country music abdicates responsibility and lionizes adolescent partying. And yet, as we have seen, country music faces head-on the frightening face of lonesomeness and embraces the creatureliness of all flesh. Perhaps no single career in country—or in any popular—music is as emblematic of maturity and the acknowledgment of tragedy as Johnny Cash's. Unlike Hank Williams, Cash lived well beyond age twenty-nine. We have Cash's wilder, carefree songs of a young man on record. But we also have the songs of a middle-aged man admitting and regretting the damage he has done. Most majestically, we have the five American Recordings made in his twilight years.[35] These albums (released from 1994 to 2006) are nothing less than testaments of dying, and dying well. The once granite voice, a Rock of Gibraltar of sound, has weakened and wavered, clogged with phlegm. In his cover of Trent Reznor's "Hurt," Cash the mature democratic American confesses that pursuits of wealth and fame have in the end produced only an "empire of dirt." He recognizes that everyone he cares for "goes away in the end" and that time wounds and breaks even the most self-sufficient.[36]

Cash's courage shines even brighter in his own songs, such as "The Man Comes Around."[37] In this extraordinarily poetic and biblically saturated piece, a Cash mere years if not months or days from death calls all human creatures to "hear the trumpets, hear the pipers" and be ready to account for our lives in the judgment dock of mortality. We are not gods making our own reality, but creatures who must responsibly engage a reality bigger than us and our best (not to mention our worst) dreams. "It's hard for thee to kick against the pricks," the truth-telling troubadour sings. The just and the unjust will be sorted out. Johnny Cash's Christian faith and mature virtue gave him the strength to admit lonesomeness, need, and vulnerability. At the last, it granted him the boldness to go eye-to-eye with death, the ultimate limitation and our starkest reminder of the inescapably tragic nature of creaturely existence. Democracy for grown-ups, indeed.

Chapter 3

Holiness and Hedonism

*I*n country music, holiness is the pork to hedonism's beans. However each might do without the other, the two go together. The vast majority of country musicians, like southerners in general, were and still are reared in the church. Their earliest public performances occur under a steeple. When they grow up and spend their Saturday nights playing honky-tonks, they may not regularly make it to church on Sunday mornings. But few denounce or throw over their faith. They are indelibly marked by it.

So Hank Williams, as dissolutely as he lived and died, recorded gospel songs and was buried with a Bible in his hand. Johnny Cash early in his career pledged a "tithe" for his recordings—one of every ten songs would be a sacred or gospel number.[1] That never stopped him from living rough and singing rougher, as when he belted out to an audience of convicts lines like "I shot that bad bitch down."[2] Red Foley's repertoire could move almost seamlessly from "Just a Closer Walk with Thee" ("Grant it, Jesus, hear my plea") to "Pinball Boogie" ("You rattle and you shake it 'til it gets in the hole").[3] Jimmie Davis would ascend to alpine heights of respectability, singing gospel songs and even becoming governor of Louisiana, but he first became known through more earthy ditties. The most famous of his bawdy numbers is the hilarious "Red Nightgown Blues," which features a nymphomaniac so sexed up she won't wear more than lingerie for her wedding. She begs the "parson" to speed up the ceremony—"Two more minutes and I'll go wrong." She chases her less enthusiastic groom around the honeymoon haven, crying, "You're my meat, you son of a gun." He escapes but she apprehends him in a haystack and ravishes him so furiously the straw ignites.[4]

Some musicians have been more disturbed than others by the collision of holiness and hedonism in their lifestyles and work. The Pentecostal Jerry Lee Lewis was kicked out of Bible school after his rousing boogie-woogie rendition of "My God Is Real" in the school chapel. Attacks of conscience later had Lewis almost abandon the recording of "Great Balls of Fire."[5] Yet surely the most tortured of country singing souls was Alabaman Ira Louvin, the high tenor in the exquisite Louvin Brothers harmonies. Ira vacillated between honkytonking and promises to buy a tent and take to the road as an evangelist. He penned and performed preachy songs such as "Broadminded," inveighing against drinking and social dancing. Constantly tormented, he might in the same set smash his mandolin onstage.[6] The alcoholic Ira would perform in a bar, revile himself for it, then drink himself into a stupor. He attempted to strangle his third wife with a telephone cord. He died, inebriated, in a head-on car wreck in 1965 (also killing his fourth wife). In a tableau like some tragicomic scene from an absurdist play, Ira's corpse ended up half in and half out of the car, knees on the pavement and elbows and head slumped on the seat. It looked as if he were praying.[7]

Of course, the clash between holiness and hedonism is not unique to country musicians, or even to the South. The United States is a puzzle to the rest of the world because of its apparently contradictory combination of fervent religiosity and an at least equally fervent materialism and coarse popular culture. It is at once the most churchgoing and the most intently comfort- and pleasure-seeking of "developed" countries. I suspect there are few better ways to get at this key and characteristic tension than through further examination of America's southern accent and country music. The South, after all, remains the most intensely religious region in the nation. And while other genres of popular culture combine degrees of holiness and hedonism, none hangs on to and honors its Christian roots so tenaciously as country music. In this chapter I will focus on the holiness aspect, especially on how American religion has taken shape culturally in ways that rob historical Christianity of its substantial prophetic power, and suggest how the Christian American pursuit of both holiness and hedonism fairly or unfairly invites charges of hypocrisy.

~~~~~~~

From its roots, and certainly at its founding as a nation, the United States was marked by religious pluralism. The original thirteen colonies all had Christian provenance, but with considerable variance: Dutch Reformed in New York, Congregationalist in Massachusetts and Connecticut, Baptist in Rhode Island, Roman Catholic in Maryland, Episcopal in Virginia, and Quaker in Pennsylvania.[8] Even this degree of pluralism made early America as a unified Christian theocracy impossible. Baptists in Rhode Island and Quakers in Pennsylvania wanted faith kept on a strictly voluntary basis and accordingly eschewed governmental endorsements of Christianity as a state religion. Clearly Catholics in Maryland and Congregationalists in New England could not profoundly agree on the ideal shape of church-state relations. The Maryland Catholics would have accorded Rome far more authority in matters of faith and polity than would have Massachusetts Congregationalists (to put it lightly).

By the time of the nation's establishment, the founders struggled to create a government that would accommodate real religious differences. Rising in the wake of the Enlightenment, this America was greatly influenced by deism. Deism centered on an amorphous deity who creates a clockwork world and then leaves it to tick away on its own power. It glossed religious differences by explicitly eschewing the details of biblical revelation and hewing to a minimum of theological beliefs, all ostensibly apparent to unaided human reason.[9] These minimal beliefs included the existence of a creator God, an innate moral law, and judgment after death for conduct in this life. In retrospect, it is clear that deism's minimal tenets were not self-evident or free of the "taint" of particular revelation. Ironically, they "were in fact derived from Christianity, the faith in which the deists themselves had been reared."[10] Hence it is not at all obvious to today's nonbelievers in biblical faith that God exists, that a coherent moral law guides all sane and reasonable humans, and that all mortals will face judgment after death. We need but recall that the eighteenth century was an age moving away from biblical religions, while still in many ways rooted in them. So even radicals such as Tom Paine agreed with fellow deists like Thomas Jefferson and Ben Franklin that a moral society could not be sustained without belief in God and expectation of judgment in life after death.[11]

The paradox, then, was that only a deism surreptitiously thickened by unacknowledged biblical revelation and attitudes could affirm as much as it did. But paint thinner not only thickens when mixed with paint. It also—true to its name—thins the paint with which it is mixed. Likewise, at the same time that it implicitly gave more substance to deism, historic Christianity was itself diluted. As it turned out, the mixture was not stable. Accordingly, deism was historically short-lived, giving way eventually to a more robust, revelation-based Christianity on the one hand and a full-scale atheism on the other hand. To put the matter starkly, the deistic Creator recognized in the Declaration of Independence is now dead, and has been for more than a century. The church still looks to the God of biblical faith, but there is no simple or straightforward connection between that living God and the short-lived God of deism—the God so important to the founders' compromises and consensus on religion and its role in national life.[12]

The real or more official Christianization of America then occurred not in the era of the nation's founding, but with the revivals of the Second and Third Great Awakenings (roughly 1800 through the 1830s and the 1880s into the first decade of the twentieth century). As historian Richard Hughes notes, at the nation's founding, Jefferson and others deists would not have carried the day without the support of free-church Christians (including Baptists and Methodists) who allied with them to abolish religious establishment by the state. Politics, as so often, made for strange bedfellows. And once the practice of religious freedom had gained a sure foothold, the free churchers wanted out of bed with the deists. Fearing just how extensive religious and moral pluralism might become, the dissenting or free-church Christians now made common cause with those in the traditions of state-established churches.[13] Concurrent especially with the Second Great Awakening, these developments marked the first real and unadulterated attempts to make America an explicitly Christian—even evangelical—nation. The revivals of the Second (and later the Third) Great Awakening were especially potent in the American South. This revivification, combined with the antagonisms of the Civil War, heightened the South's sense of itself as the last standing redoubt of Christianity in the civilized world. Southern pastors cast the war as a struggle not merely between Confederates and Unionists, or slaveholders and abolitionists, but as a faceoff of heaven and hell on earth. As one South Carolina pulpiteer put it, the war matched "atheists, socialists, communists, red republicans, Jacobins on the one side" and true Christianity with its "order and regulated freedom" on the other side.[14]

Evangelicalism was strongest through the South, but enjoyed prominence close to national cultural and educational centers of power into the twentieth century. Princeton Theological Seminary was the last elite, Ivy League institution to turn away from conservative evangelicalism. Arguments over biblical criticism and evolution especially, with Freudian psychology and Marxism as other towering antagonists of much of evangelicalism, eventually won the day for modernism among American gatekeepers of thought and opinion. J. Gresham Machen, the last defender of conservative evangelicalism at Princeton, departed that institution in 1929, four years after the Scopes trial and its attendant publicity humiliated creationist evangelicals across the nation. From the Civil War and even before, as mentioned, the South saw itself as the final redoubt of genuine Christianity. By the 1930s historical events manifestly appeared to confirm its self-image as an island of Christendom in the United States.[15]

Contiguity and migration from the southern states spread the South's mini-Christendom to the Southwest. Revivalism and attendant crusades for moral and religious legislation were strong in that region. So Oklahoma, achieving statehood in 1907, was "born sober," with state constitutional provisions banning alcohol, and would not approve liquor by the drink until 1985. In the South and Southwest there existed a kind of "evangelical establishment" that framed community standards. As James Gregory writes,

> The pluralism which permitted subgroups to maintain a variety of moral, religious, and ethnic perspectives in Western and Northern

cities flourished only weakly in Southwestern urban areas and not at all in small town and rural settings, where as one Missourian put it, the churches "control everything." What they controlled was not so much behavior as the standards by which behavior was evaluated.[16]

Opinionmakers characteristically—and erroneously—assigned American evangelicalism to the tomb. In national terms, evangelicals did retreat from politics and public visibility from the 1930 until the 1970s. But their institutions remained powerful, if circumscribed, in the South and Southwest. And there were key outposts in the North, such as the Chicago area's Moody Bible Institute and Wheaton College. The wide and deep popular strength of southern evangelicalism decisively connected with northern pockets of evangelicalism when the North Carolina-born Billy Graham attended and graduated from Wheaton College during World War II. Evangelist Graham surged to national prominence in 1949, after newspaper mogul William Randolph Hearst drew attention to Graham's Los Angeles revival meetings. The evangelist was then at the nexus of the development of several crucial institutional births and resurrections beginning in the 1950s. Graham was a key player in the birth of *Christianity Today* magazine, the organization of the National Association of Evangelicals, and a catalyst for the advancement of evangelical colleges and seminaries. In regard not least to the resurgence of evangelicalism nationally, the seeds for the southernization of America were planted and carefully cultivated decades before Jerry Falwell's Moral Majority burst onto the scene in 1979.

∗∗∗∗∗∗∗

Currently the de facto Protestant mainline in the United States is evangelicalism. It is not older mainline Protestants, such as United Methodists, Presbyterians, and Lutherans[17] who enjoy regular access to Congress and the White House, but evangelical leaders such as James Dobson and organizations such as the National Association of Evangelicals. In power centers as well much of its heartland, America speaks with a southern, evangelical accent.

The resurgence of evangelicalism is an aspect or inflection of the success of the Republicans' Southern Strategy that deserves more attention here. In chapter 1, I underscored the tactics of racism, resentment, and division that mark the Southern Strategy. These factors are important and demand both notice and repudiation. At the same time, it will not do to see the Republican Party's appropriation of culture and faith as purely cynical and manipulative. The Christian presences and influences in America's history and present are variegated and often confused, but they are real and significant. Nor have these Christian presences and influences been simply and unaccountably aggressive (or actively regressive) since the 1970s. The Democrats have not merely been tone-deaf to the breadth of culture and religion's centrality to culture. They have in certain respects opted for religious perspectives at odds not merely with conservative evangelicalism but with historic and orthodox Christianity more generally.[18]

Recall our earlier discussion of religion most broadly as that to which people assign their "ultimate concern." As the locus and catalyst of a culture's ultimate concern, religion provides a comprehensive sense of that culture's creation and final direction, its roots and destiny. Such comprehensive visions need not be explicitly theological; some are, in fact, forthrightly secular. Now turn the clock back to 1972. Then the Republican Party was (in religious terms) dominated by the old mainline—the established and at least moderately progressive Protestant denominations including Methodists, Episcopalians, Lutherans, black Baptists, and Presbyterians. Evangelicals and Roman Catholics, with the working classes in general, were largely Democratic voters. But leading up to the 1972 Democratic National Convention, Democratic strategists determined that the "party's [future] political self-interest" lay in appealing to other constituencies.[19] Desperate to end the Vietnam War and suspicious of racism in conventionally religious circles, the strategists deliberately turned to the more consistently progressive constituency of secularists—self-identifed agnostics, atheists, and persons who seldom or never attended church or synagogue. Consequently, more than 33 percent of the white delegates at the 1972 Democratic National Convention were secularists (this when only about five percent of the entire national population was so identified.)[20]

Subsequently these strategists and their successors arranged delegate selection to favor secularists and secularist representation. Perhaps most significantly, the party made a pro-choice stance a litmus test for participation and influence at the party's center. Of course many Democrats remained pro-life through the 1970s, but from 1976 onward, every serious Democratic presidential candidate has stood in favor of legalized, broadly available abortion. By 1992, pro-life Pennsylvania Governor Robert Casey was denied an opportunity to address the Democratic National Convention on the subject of abortion. In 2004, the organization Democrats for Life was not allowed to link its Web site to the Democratic National Committee's Web site.[21] The abortion issue presents its own complications and nuances, but the Christian church from its inception has been wary of abortion.[22] The Democratic Party's doctrinaire and sometimes radical position for abortion on demand has been a key factor driving Roman Catholics, evangelicals, and other orthodox Christians away from the party and its ballots. (To take but one example from our focal realm of country music, bluegrass performer Ricky Skaggs has stated bluntly, "When the Democrats quit voting to kill babies, I might have an ear for what they have to say.")[23]

More generally, as noted above, the Democrats in a sense opted for an alternative religious stance, that of agnostic secularism. They grossly miscalculated the ongoing endurance of traditional faiths in America. They consistently evinced an inability to see Christianity, Judaism, Islam, or other anciently rooted faiths as primary realities, with adherents who made determinative decisions about their lives according to those faiths. They tended instead to view all "conventional" religion as epiphenomena, merely the waves and ripples radiating out from secular political or economic stones, rather than taking traditional religions as splash-making rocks in their own right.

The subsequent polarization on religion and such issues as abortion has left many American Christians (along with other traditional religionists) in an unhappy and untenable position. Many—and I include myself in their number—worry over the American right's tendency to valorize military solutions to most international difficulties and to pander to the interests of big business while effectively ignoring the welfare of minorities. Yet the American left, the Democratic Party most particularly, has stubbornly disallowed the importance and reality of traditional faith, and has made little room for differences on such controversial issues as abortion. It is unfortunately true—and should never be forgotten—that many southerners and evangelicals long resisted civil rights for African Americans. But the Democratic Party resolutely ignored the vitally Christian roots of that same movement for civil rights. A distinctly different scenario was possible. History might have unfolded differently if the Democratic Party had honored Christian constituencies no less than their avowedly secular constituencies. Theologian Charles Marsh ably summarizes such a possibility in a discernment worth quoting at length:

> Martin Luther King Jr. had spoken in judgment of the liberal establishment in his denunciations of Vietnam and the American culture of violence. His comprehensive devotion to the sacredness of life would have surely included abortion, or risked grave inconsistency. After hearing the Supreme Court decision [of *Roe vs. Wade*, 1973], Fannie Lou Hamer, who had been forcibly sterilized in her twenties, had remarked, "Now they're starting to kill black babies." The disproportionate number of aborted black babies to white in the South could be claimed by white liberals as a demonstration of social compassion only by mocking the civil rights movement's protections of society's most excluded and vulnerable. Reverend Ed King of the Mississippi Freedom Democratic Party had taken the Supreme Court decision as an expression of the "anti-poor policies of the Republican President, Richard Nixon," an insidious and now legal way of achieving massive cuts in welfare spending by "cutting down on black welfare babies."
>
> But white conservative Christians could not share the civil rights movement's outrage at *Roe vs. Wade* because most white Christians had really never cared about black babies to begin with. Lacking a commitment to the poor and the excluded, conservative white opposition to abortion produced nothing so much as a generation of pious patriots; and, as it turned out, any action would be justified in waging war against abortion except support of precisely those social policies for the poor that would make abortion less desirable.[24]

In later chapters we will return to discussion of a Christian faith with historical awareness of its Scripture and traditions, one that is careful to retain a keen concern for the outcast and easily excluded. For now it is important to clarify and elaborate on the genuine religious concerns of the southern-rooted conservative evangelicalism now so influential in the nation's public affairs. I have said that various antagonists of conservative or traditional religious presence in public life have tended to dismiss faith as a core reality. There is an inclination to credit material (or economic) and raw, power-hungry politics as the "real" bases and motivators of those who say their activism is religiously motivated. Religion, and specifically conservative Christianity, is then viewed as an epiphenomenon, not as a primary phenomenon or reality in its own right. And it is imagined to be merely instrumental—a tool, witting or unwitting—wielded to achieve other, supposedly deeper aims and ends.

Thus, for instance, Robert Kennedy Jr., in his otherwise admirable work on behalf of environmental conservation, has averred that conservative evangelical opposition to conservation policies is not actually religiously motivated. Instead, "With the fundamentalists, it's all about power."[25] I share Kennedy's opposition to evangelicals who dismiss global warming and display carelessness about stewardship of God's creation. But I think it a dire misconstrual to downplay the motivating and determinative potency of religious faith on environmental and other important public matters. The southern-accented Christian faith of millions of Americans is real and primary—they answer to a God whom they believe to be really, objectively "there" and other than themselves. The secularist tendency to treat faith as at best an epiphenomenon and an instrumental or secondary good fails to understand the devout as they understand themselves.[26] It undercuts ground for honest and lucid, if still intense, disagreement. More crucially, especially for the theological social critic, it obscures and removes important theological issues from debate and discussion. If these Christians are really moved by naked power or a veiled economic self-interest, there is no need to argue and try to correct their mistaken theological convictions. Then politically involved evangelicals are merely lackeys or hypocrites, and the more foundational (self-interested economic and political) matters supposedly motivating them demand immediate engagement.

But if hypocrisy is not the main resort for explaining and engaging misguided evangelical (and other religious) politics, how do we account for the apparent Great American Contradiction of holiness and hedonism? It is a fact that roughly the same divorce rates mark people of America's Bible Belt as mark its coastal and secular elites. Rates of violence on the unborn (abortion) and the already born (murder, rape, robbery, etc.) in religious American regions are as high as or higher than in the professedly secular or irreligious territories. Corporate greed is rampant in religious circles (such as the evangelical Kenneth Lay's Enron) and not just on a godless Wall Street. If hedonistic "me-first" attitudes contribute to such behaviors, they are embodied by Americans generally, including those of religious conviction.

The blanket judgment of hypocrisy dissolves the baffling but real tension of Americans being intensely committed to both holiness and hedonism. Then holiness is only apparent or even duplicitous, and the professedly Christian Americans are at best simply and grossly deluded, at worst cynical and exploitative deceivers. Theology, and faith, are consequently not taken seriously. They are dismissed.

An alternative reading of the holiness-hedonism puzzle begins with a reconsideration of what we mean by hypocrisy. In its strictest meaning, hypocrisy derives from a Greek theatrical term. The actor may quite convincingly inhabit his character, but he knows the character is not him—he is playing a role from which he can and does detach himself. A role is readily discarded when it no longer serves a purpose. Country musicians such as Hank Williams and Ira Louvin, torn as they were between holiness and hedonism, were authentically possessed by Christian conviction. They did not include sacred songs in their performances simply to play a role. If so, they would have been much less tortured by the tensions inherent to their lifestyles. Like other southerners, they were reared in a kind of Christianity, imbibing it with mother's milk and no more ready or capable of dismissing it from their lives than they were of wanting Mama dead and forgotten.

In this regard I have already mentioned not only Williams and Lou-vin, but the mercurial rocker and country singer Jerry Lee Lewis. Jerry Lee merits more attention. In his case, the pervasiveness of bone-deep faith and the inescapability of a really existing and acting God in the southern character burns with the intense clarity of a prairie fire on a moonless night.

Reared by a devout Assemblies of God mother (and a moonshiner father), Lewis was formed by an evangelical Pentecostal Christianity unafraid of ecstatic emotion and its bodily expression. Pentecostal worship taps into a liturgical line flowing directly from the camp meetings and revivals of the nineteenth century. At those revivals men and women were so overcome by the power of the Spirit that they barked up trees like dogs, laughed uncontrollably, shook, shouted, wept, and collapsed into the dirt as if shot dead. Jerry Lee Lewis is a descendant of this stock, a practitioner of these traditions. There are various ways we might reduce and dismiss such phenomena. We can speak of nervous catharsis, of mass hypnosis and excitation, and notice such outbursts in a variety of religions. But the point is that from the tongues-speaking apostles in the New Testament down to Jerry Lee Lewis, those overtaken by such experiences sensed them-selves confronted and consumed by something beyond themselves, bigger than themselves—a force, a spirit, a power that lifted and car-ried them away like leaves in a gale. This overcoming or possession was, in short, not something they created or elicited, not something they could control and direct.

Lewis's extraordinary power as a performer rose from his Pente-costal training at letting himself go, in casting aside all worries about sobriety or dignity, all pretensions at poise or polish, and surrendering himself to whatever spirit was unleashed. Such surrender takes a kind of spiritual courage, the courage of a bullrider who descends onto the back of a half-ton wild animal and abandons himself to its unpre-dictable and volcanic strength. Imperiling all bodily well-being, the bullrider enacts a philosophical proposition: "This is life, in eight sec-onds, and all any of us can really do is hang on." You can witness Jerry Lee dangling and bouncing on the back of the beast again and again in his thrilling music, but perhaps nowhere more outstandingly than in the 1964 recording of his gig at the Star Club in Hamburg, Germany.

Lewis barrels out of the concert's gate at full speed and blazes relentlessly through "Mean Woman Blues," "Money," and five more of his standards. Then he takes a breath, if only slightly, on the ballad-paced "Your Cheatin' Heart." From there he dives back into two more full-bore rockers, spiced with his trademark piano pumping and slashing, falling into surging rhythms as inexorable as the tides, vocalizing not only with discernibly sung words but with hums, growls, hiccups, laughter in melody, tiger purrs, and shouts of reckless gibberish (rock and roll glossolalia?). He climaxes the evening with his first hit, "Whole Lotta Shakin' Goin' On."

From the first note of the first song, he has played the crowd as mercilessly as his piano. Still, driven into a fever, the ecstatic audience can only want more. Now Jerry Lee leads them and his desperately flailing drummer and guitarists into the home stretch. After three rousing refrains, he tells them what they have surely already guessed, that, "Baby, really got the bull by the horns." Then he cools the tempo for a full minute and one-half, teasing, "Easy now . . . Ease it on down . . . ," before he at last whiplashes ("Let's go one time!") back into full speed and rips the lyrics into vocal shreds. Flogging the piano like a dying horse just short of water, he drags band and listeners through the closing bars with hoarsely urgent exhortations: "Come on! Come on!" The audience lets go with all manner of rocking concert approval, including German-accented chants of "Jer-ree, Jer-ree, Jer-ree," and overtakes the band in noise level, while Lewis chord-slams the piano out of its misery. Then we hear Lewis's final words on the album. Sounding surprised and dizzy from the ride, he exhales two rollercoasting, rising and falling exclamations— "Whoooaaaahhhhhh, whooooooaahhh." So it has been a ride, even for Jerree. He is not so much the master or artisan of his performance as he is himself its object and vehicle. He has only abandoned himself, and hung on as long as he could.[27]

The formal resemblance to a Pentecostal worship service is patent, and Lewis himself was haunted by how closely his rock concert abandon mimicked his churchly ecstasy. Even saints and theologians cannot exactly parse just where the possession by the Holy Spirit ends and susceptibility to other spirits—of benign merriment or chemical inducement, or of hysteria, darkness, and the demonic—

begins; and Lewis was no theologian. But he had no doubt about the objectivity or reality of transcendent powers. And unlike more sophisticated minds, he had no illusions that he could command or control these powers.

In Memphis, Sun Studio, 1957, Jerry Lee and Sam Phillips were preparing to record what would become one of Lewis's standards, "Great Balls of Fire." As in many of Lewis's songs, the sexual double entendre of this song is obvious enough. While reading over the song's lead sheet, Lewis apparently had a different, religious association dawn on him. The "Great Balls of Fire" might not only symbolize sexual excitement, but also suggest the flames of apocalyptic judgment. The tape is already rolling, and Jerry Lee balks at proceeding. He's not sure he can perform this song because he has thought of this final accounting, and it reminds him of a horrible reality whose name he will not speak, but can only spell out emphatically: "H-E-L-L." It is fine and good to "make merry to the joy of God," he tells Sam Phillips, but rock and roll is impure and "worldly music." Phillips fervently attempts to persuade Lewis he can be both a rock and roll "exponent" and a Christian. Lewis agrees that you can "do good" and have "a kind heart" without Christ's empowerment. Thinking his argument has gained critical momentum, Phillips then declares, "You can save souls!" Jerry is shocked, flabbergasted: he clearly respects "Mr. Phillips," but now the famed producer is speaking self-evident nonsense. He might just as well be trying to convince Lewis that up is down or left is right or that the sun sets in the east. Jerry Lee can only shout back, as if the flooding waters of meaningless chaos have pooled around his feet and are rising above his knees: "No! NO, NO, NO!" Then: "How can the devil save souls? . . . I have the devil in me. If I didn't, I'd be a Christian."

We need not cede to Lewis the point that the rock and roll or any other spirit must be necessarily of the Lord *or* of the devil. The point, in considering the southern character and allegations of hypocrisy, is that Jerry Lee inhabits *both* the profane world (Saturday night) *and* the sacred world (Sunday morning) and that, for him, neither one is unreal or untrue. How much simpler, not to say relaxing, to be nothing but a hypocrite, knowingly if mendaciously and exploitatively acting the role of a believer. Lewis is compelled to play rock music,

yes, but no less convinced that it is the devil's music and that performing it takes him within scorching range of the fires of hell.
Phillips wants to ease the tension, to adjust Lewis's perceptions or
beliefs about Christianity, or rock, or both, but Phillips's attempted
tweaking strikes Lewis as the equivalent of the world turning upside
down. "Mr. Phillips," he insists. "I don't care. It ain't what you
believe, it's what's written in the Bible. . . . It's what is *there*, Mr.
Phillips." Two plus two equals four. Dogs don't get along with cats.
Humans tread the earth, birds fly. What's written in the Bible is "what
is *there*," no more liable to change or manipulation than any other
gross and basic reality. Jerry Lee might like to wish away God and
the biblical cosmos, and just play his rattling piano and gratify all
impulses guilt free, but that ain't what's written. Jerry Lee Lewis is
not so much a hypocrite as a walking contradiction.[28]

Similar dynamics were at work at the 2006 Academy Awards.
There the rap group Three 6 Mafia, hailing from Memphis, won the
Oscar for best song with their candidly titled "It's Hard Out Here for
a Pimp." In a rambling acceptance speech, the rappers thanked not
only Mom and family and their record company, but Jesus. The rapper's public cachet (unlike the country singer's) is not enhanced by
profession of religious convictions, and a group now more famous
than ever for a song empathizing with pimping need not go out of its
way to credit Jesus with its success. But for Three 6 Mafia, Kanye
West, Lauryn Hill, and other rappers with southern roots, religion and
religion's objects are real. If this reality may sometimes awkwardly
comport with their lyrics or public behavior, it nevertheless marks
who and what they are. They cannot discard it like a role in a play that
has had its run.

For such hip-hoppers and other black musicians with southern
roots, as for Jerry Lee on the white side of the tracks, life would be
much easier if they were simply hypocrites. Consider the great soul
singer Marvin Gaye, reared as a preacher's kid, practically praying in
songs scattered through his classic album *What's Going On*, inscrib-
ing in the liner notes of his final albums statements such as "I still love
Jesus"—but also and all along passionate for unbridled sex and sen-
suality, seductively purring "Let's Get It On" and graphically extolling
"Sexual Healing." Gaye would have passed his tumultuous life with

less agony if he didn't really mean it about either the church (Sunday morning) or the hedonistic sex (Saturday night). But he could give up neither, seeing life as "a paradox between Jesus and pussy."[29]

⚡⚡⚡⚡⚡⚡⚡

What is true for the southern music world holds as well for southern-accented political and social involvement. It is not all and simply the ravings of hypocrites. The Christianity is (very often) genuine and indelible. Where we disagree with it, we do not get very far by supposing it to be mere posturing and manipulative pretense. Seen in serious theological perspective, there are at least three possibilities for what is truly going on when purportedly Christian musicians or politicians prove themselves susceptible to the allures of hedonism even as they pursue holiness.

The first possibility is outright, genuine hypocrisy. In arguing that our public debate often moves too quickly and grossly to an assumption of hypocrisy, I am not pretending there is no such category at all. There have been, are, and will be many more cases of people who play Christianity as a role, who go through the motions of a few (highly visible) Christian practices and speak the Christian patois with familiarity, but who really have no interest in the pursuit of holiness for its own sake. These are the politicians or other public figures who pretend to faith for exploitation's sake—to collect more votes, draw a bigger market share, or otherwise gain coincidental benefits of faith without actually being faithful. This is cynical, direct instrumentalization of religion, using faith as a tool just as a burglar employs a device to pick locks. Devout Christians should be even more offended by outright, exploitative hypocrisy than are secularists.

The second possibility is a faith genuinely held, but gone astray. Here faith has been an authentic aim and motivation. But somewhere along the way other ultimate aims or aspirations or irresistible desires have overtaken faith and distorted it. Gradually it has become more important to gain or retain power, to protect reputation, to gratify personal lusts, than it is to stand faithful, to serve the living God in all things. In theological terms, this possibility presents the grievous danger of idolatry. The ugly (but outwardly attractive) head of idolatry has reared itself whenever Christianity is reduced to and identified with particular and partial interests, so that "true Christianity" is reserved for those who are Americans, or of the upper class, or Republican or Democrat. Here too faith is instrumentalized, but not cynically and with full intentionality. In this case the most effective challenge can be theological, and may come from other Christians. It involves work to persuade misguided Christians that they are, in fact, misguided—that they have lost sight of the living Christ, the true faith.

The third possibility is a faith genuinely held and earnestly honored, but not lived up to always and absolutely. Here the believer caught in contradiction is not a rank hypocrite and has not succumbed or habituated himself or herself to idolatry, but has stumbled. In theological terms, we are talking about sin, and all persons—including believers—are continually susceptible to it. Full perfection or absolute holiness will never be achieved this side of the eschaton. Sin until then may be inevitable and implacable, but that does not make it commendable or trivial. Sinfulness is a condition to be acknowledged but not serenely accepted. By Christian understanding, sin is like a chronic disease: it is best admitted and taken account of, yet to live you must fight it until the day you die. So in the case of sin, the way forward is one of humility and emendation, repeated as necessary.

In short, the real hypocrite is the man who actually regards his bride with indifference or disdain, but marries for the money. The idolater acts with some genuine affection, but would never wed a poor woman even if she otherwise possessed the same qualities as his wealthy bride. The sinner first and foremost loves his bride for who and what she is, and commits for better and for worse, but remains liable to straying and failure.

Homely metaphors aside, these basic theological considerations, if recognized and more regularly employed, can help all Americans better to understand and respond to the Great American Contradiction of holiness and hedonism. Even those who regard Christian convictions as illusory will better communicate with their Christian fellow citizens if they allow that these devout citizens, at least, take faith seriously, as directed to a real and living God, as the most determining and important factor in how they live and die. Then the non-Christian citizen can still identify hypocrisy in certain cases, yet not automatically end conversation or debate by disallowing all possibility of the professed (if sometimes inconsistent) Christian as something other than a rank and callous manipulator, engaging the language and practice of faith as nothing more than a shell game. Furthermore, the non-Christian citizen arguing with a Christian fellow citizen might recognize that for Christians idolatry is a worse offense than hypocrisy. To instrumentalize faith or take the living God's "name in vain" is a violation of the First Commandment, and chief among the sins judged harshly in Scripture. Call me a hypocrite, and, if I am a genuine Christian, I am simply reminded that I may be inconsistent and a garden-variety sinner. Call me an idolater, and I had better really examine myself and my actions, for fear that I may have slipped into the most grievous and destructive sin of all.

∞∞∞∞∞∞∞

Relatedly, for us who profess Christianity, reflection on the characteristic American contradiction of holiness and hedonism is a pointed reminder that in our public as well as our private relations, in our politics as well as in our hearts, we are sinners. We may know we are not really hypocrites, but can often act just like rank hypocrites. Even more importantly, we can slip into a sin deeper and graver than that any real hypocrite can achieve: we may become idolaters.

Because idolatry is the most destructive of sinful conditions, the greatest danger to the true faithfulness of the American church comes not from without but from within. That danger is not persecution or victimization or accusations of hypocrisy, but our own all-too-easy tendency to sentimentalize our faith. To sentimentalize the faith is to instrumentalize it, to make it a tool of our ambitions, our comfort, and our security. Sentimentalization is mild-mannered idolatry, sin sweetened and trivialized. Sentimentality kills vital faith with bland complacency.

Biblically, faith can be onerous and difficult. Moses did not want to go back to Egypt, even though God sent him. Then, once freed, the Israelites wanted to return to the "fleshpots" of Egypt rather than wander after God in the wilderness. The Jews have understandably and wisely recognized that being the chosen people is more a challenge and a sometimes crushing weight than it is a carefree privilege or cheerful entitlement. Jesus, himself a faithful Jew, wanted desperately not to take up the cross that confronted him. In so many ways, as Peter counseled, judgment begins with the household of God (1 Peter 4:17). Christians who live under real persecution, and in much less affluent circumstances than most contemporary American Christians, have little trouble recognizing and remembering that true faith contributes only incidentally, if at all, to complacency and comfort.

Those of us who do live in affluent and comparatively comfortable circumstances, however, are prone to domesticate and sentimentalize faith. Whenever we cannot imagine faith as a burden and instead begin to presume it as "a self-righteous claim to some privileged moral status," we are sentimentalizing faith.[30] Sentimentalization is not counteracted best with a dismissal of all faith (no one lives without a religion of one kind or another), but with renewed commitment to a faith that is honest and shriven of triumphalism. This faith recognizes that America, no matter how powerful monetarily or militarily, is not the church. It admits that we are all creatures and sinners. It asks sacrifices primarily of ourselves and our own, not of children in bedraggled, distant nations or "aliens" in our midst. It is wary of all scapegoating. Inasmuch as it sees faith as two-edged sword, it remembers that the sharpest and most prophetic edge is directed inward and not outward.

Such a faith can embrace the American democracy for grown-ups that recognizes limits, accepts accountability, and practices a humility demanding more courage than any breast-pounding jingoism or demonizing attack. Johnny Cash exemplified just such an honest, humble, and unsentimental faith. Cash was a Christian who could erupt in violence, succumb to drugs and fornication and national chauvinism, give in to the racist tendencies of his upbringing, but rarely denied or sentimentalized his sinfulness. Accordingly, he could empathize with convicts as fellow "rebels, outsiders, and miscreants." After Jamaican youths brutally robbed the Cash home on Christmas of 1982, Cash commented, "We had a kinship, they and I: I knew how they thought, I knew how they needed. They were like me."[31]

Cash's music is marked and re-marked by an unsentimental faith, by his recognition of himself as a sinner in need of ongoing redemption. Performing a song written about him by a former son-in-law, he confessed a "beast in me," a troubled sinfulness sometimes only barely caged by "frail and fragile bars." This prowling, crouching lion might sometimes almost convince him that it had vanished "in the air"—then, especially, he "must beware of the beast in me."[32]

Here is another example of Cash's unsentimental faith. In a simple but striking country gospel song, he narrates slipping into the back of church late one evening just as a worship service is winding up with testimonies. One congregant crows that he is going to heaven as straight and fast as an arrow sprung from a bow. A second boasts that he's gliding into paradise "like a giant clipper ship." A third takes to his feet and proclaims, "I'm flying on silver wings, sailing over all the troubles and trials down below." Then a little old lady in a back pew stands up, and looks not at the preacher or the congregation, but raises her face toward heaven and addresses God. She can claim no rapid and direct transit to heaven. She is aware that she passes through clouds and is "stumbling on the way"—"By my mistakes," she confesses, "I barely make a half a mile a day." But if she heeds Christ and his way, "Even I might get to heaven at a half a mile a day."[33]

"*Even* I . . ." Even you and I, rich and secure and comfortable American Christians?

Chapter 4

Tradition and Progress

*T*he United States considers itself at once the most traditional and the most modern and progressive of Western—or any other—countries. It is famously religious and fills church pews at rates far eclipsing those of European countries and of Canada, its neighbor to the north. It is explicitly and often officially preoccupied with "traditional values." America resists the welfare state more vigorously than its northern neighbor and European allies. And in international comparative terms the United States has in its past and present next to nothing resembling socialist or "leftist" political parties. In all these ways it is proudly and quite stubbornly traditional.

At the same time, the United States was born of a revolution and persistently considers itself at the global vanguard of liberalism (in the sense of the historical movement for maximizing individual liberty and freedom). The eminent political theologian Oliver O'Donovan marks the First Amendment of the U.S. Constitution—with its prohibition of the state establishment of religion—as the "symbolic end of Christendom."[1] In a similar vein, America distances itself especially from old-world Europe and, even two centuries plus into its history, fancies itself a nation unencumbered by the hoary complications of the past. Americans are more interested in the future than in history. When the British wit G. K. Chesterton visited here in 1921, he found New York City genuinely and "always new." Gaping among the demolished rubble of older buildings and the omnipresent scaffolding of recent construction, Chesterton averred, "A stranger might well say that the chief industry of the citizens consists of

63

destroying their city; but he soon realizes that they always start it all over again with undiminished energy and hope. At first I had a fancy that they never quite finished putting up a big building without feeling it was time to pull it down again; and that somebody began to dig up the first foundations while somebody else was putting on the last tiles." Journeying westward to Oklahoma, then only fourteen years old as a state, Chesterton found a place "proud of having no history. It is glowing with the sense of having a great future—and nothing else."[2] What was true then is true still today. Not least in its fascination with the latest technological gadgetry, America looks forward obsessively. Like a driver full-bore on a freeway, it glances behind only when jockeying into a new lane, to make sure no one is about to pass from the rear.

In his contradictory embrace of both tradition and progress, Johnny Cash was quintessentially American. As one biographer puts it, he had an "ambivalent attitude toward his roots."[3] He grew up laboring alongside his family in the cotton fields of northeastern Arkansas, and much of his music celebrated a bygone nation of primitive rural origins and upward advancement for any individual ready to work hard enough for it. But his own life story showed that lifting oneself up by one's own bootstraps not only denies the laws of physics; it also distorts American history. Cash's hometown of Dyess was established by the federal government in 1934, as a relief effort allotting parcels of land to hard-pressed migrants willing to drain and clear swampland, then raise subsistence crops of cotton and beans. J.R., as Cash was known in his youth, found it "second nature that we wouldn't live in Dyess when we were grown."[4] As one of J.R.'s peers later put it, "I don't know of hardly anyone what wanted to stay at Dyess and raise cotton."[5] Cash took off just months out of high school, first to Michigan to work on an automobile body assembly line, then soon to the Air Force and a stationing in Germany. He never again lived in Dyess. And he rarely returned for family reunions or on any other occasion, though Dyess was less than a five-hour drive from his eventual home near Nashville.

As for Nashville itself: Though by the late sixties he would be seen as the leading worldwide ambassador of country music, Cash had a love-hate relationship with its capital city. He first made his name in Memphis, that other Tennessee music city. With a sound rhythmically accentuated like rock, and a band minus either fiddle or steel guitar, he was only grudgingly welcomed on to the Grand Ole Opry stage. In some ways more comfortable with New York City's folk music scene, Cash cast himself as a folk singer early in his career. He disappeared from public view in the early 1960s, not only because he was drug-addled, but because Nashville fell in love with a "countrypolitan" sound heavy on orchestral strings and wary of any vocalization or instrumentation that might too tangibly remind listeners of the music's hillbilly origins. Johnny Cash's sound was now too traditional for the country music gatekeepers. His career was resuscitated in 1968, when Columbia Music's producer Bob Johnston, a Nashville outsider, gave the go-ahead to record Cash raw and real at Folsom Prison. Yet by the late 1970s Nashville was again relegating Cash to museum status, with first one and then a second major record company canceling his contracts. The Man in Black's subsequent and second major comeback owed little to Nashville. In 1994, Rick Rubin, a Los Angeles-based producer with rap and heavy metal credits, released Cash's first American Records album. When the album won a Grammy despite Nashville and country radio neglect, Rubin and Cash took out an ad in an industry trade magazine. It featured an old picture of an angry Cash thrusting the middle finger at a photographer, and sarcastically thanked the Music City for its support. The aging Cash spoke out against censorship of rock music, covered a song by the goth-metal band Nine Inch Nails, and with model Kate Moss bound to a chair for "Delia's Gone," made a music video too hot for MTV to air until it was recut.[6]

American music, rural and crude to its roots? But also cutting edge and ever open to the cool of tomorrow no less than the cool of yesterday? "Hello. I'm Johnny Cash." The Man in Black's art constantly grappled with the insistent American bearhug of both tradition and progress. Perhaps this is nowhere more plainly evident and more revealing than in Cash's rich corpus of train songs.

The Industrial Revolution did not begin with railroads, but, as the essayist Rebecca Solnit notes,

> railroads magnified its effects and possibilities unfathomably, and these roaring, puffing machines came to seem that revolution incarnate. Often compared to dragons, they devoured coal and iron in unprecedented quantities, spreading mines and mills wherever they went. In the United States, they ran on wood, and whole forests were fed into their boilers, as though the landscape were being devoured by speed. Railroads made possible the consolidation of industries and the industrialization of traditional activities. The fast, cheap transport of goods meant that a town could be given over to shoe-making or beer-making, a whole region to cattle raising or wheatgrowing, and people grew used to depending upon commodities that seemed to come from nowhere.[7]

That fire-breathing locomotives were often compared to dragons is an indication of how railroads compelled attention, both fascinated and fearful. Before the clattering train, all transportation was limited by powers of nature—the gallop of horses, the velocity of the blowing wind that filled sails. The locomotive was manifestly alien to nature and to the beasts of burden humans had for so long domesticated and lived with intimately. Monstrously huge and heavy, louder than any animal, invulnerable to fatigue, capable of bearing more load than a hundred mule trains, the railroad train overwhelmed all objections to its coming with wonder and with its formerly inconceivable efficiency for travel and industry. Still, hesitations crept into even adulatory comments on the great new machine. Riding on a train averaging twelve miles per hour, Ulysses S. Grant commented that it felt as if the train were "annihilating space."[8] Grant's maximally violent imagery—he has the train not "covering" or "passing through" but "annihilating" space—gestured to his sense that there was something shocking and unnatural about railroading. He and others intuited that the train, for all its manifest benefits, exacted some terrible tribute for those gifts. It devoured not only wood and coal but silence, remoteness, natural rhythms of time and movement—and with these intangibles it devoured the ways of life associated with them. After a visit to Egypt, Mark Twain claimed that Egyptian railroaders shoveled ancient mummies into the locomotives' boilers.[9] But Egypt's railroads were unique only in the literalness with which they were fueled by the past, hurtled faster into the future by obliterating history.

Of course, this ominous side of progress was at first only intuited and vaguely sensed. Any forebodings rural Americans had were overshadowed by the employment opportunities, accessible markets, and romance that trains provided. There was initially the work of constructing the railroads, followed by the chance to toil as an engineer or fireman or brakeman on the trains—all labor options that were considered alluring in comparison to farming. There were opportunities to sell farm and garden produce to distant markets. There were rocky treasures such as coal to be dug out of mountains and valleys and shipped to teeming cities. Even if one's daily bread was not earned directly via the railways, the train carried excitement and promise. Appalachian hill dwellers and Texas ranchers who before might spend weeks or months in isolation now could receive regular visitors from distant cities, and the trains made mail frequent and regular. Boredom and lonesomeness were shattered by the sight or sound of trains chugging around the bend or across the plains. And if life seemed dull or hard enough, then trains not only came to the countrysides but left them: the railroad incarnated the possibility, however faint, of escape, of better places and a sweeter life.

A preponderance of train songs in country music are devoted to this romance of the railroad. Indicating that the American attachment to speed predates the automobile, many songs praise the rapidity and power of trains. Roy Acuff's "Fireball Mail" races so fast it "sails," and, like his "Wabash Cannonball," it can "fly." "Tennessee Central (Number 9)," meanwhile, "is a-burnin' up the wind."[10] One of Cash's favorites, "The Orange Blossom Special," is the "fastest train on the line." But if a number of songs find speed itself exhilarating, it is the possibilities of speed—freedom and escape—that more often capture the musical imagination. Leadbelly's "Midnight Special" embodies liberation from prison, much as the train in Cash's "Folsom Prison Blues" is a bitter reminder that only those outside prison walls can "keep a-movin', and that's what tortures me."[11] Hank Snow in "Movin' On" suffers his lover's infidelities for the last time: it is the sound of "the big eight wheels rollin' down the track" that signals "your true-lovin' daddy ain't comin' back."[12] Notice that these trains of song need aim for no specific destination. Some can head toward terminal points both mundane (often home, as in Cash's "Hey Porter") and spiritual (as in the Cash-recorded "Life's Railway to Heaven" and "Down There by the Train"). But more typically what attracts is sheer mobility and open-ended freedom, with no definite destination. For country singers and their listeners, the train whistle often arouses the itch to ramble, as with Roy Acuff in "Freight Train Blues"—"when that whistle blows I gotta' go."[13] Jimmie Rodgers classically intones, in "Brakeman's Blues," that it may be "good times here, but it's better down the road."[14] So country train songs embrace the romance of speed, freedom, and places and times "down the road," desirable exactly because they remain in an untouched, pristine future.

Right here, then, we encounter the irony of the simultaneous American embrace of both tradition and progress. Country music is considered a highly traditional music, and train songs are at its heart. These very songs, especially now that rail passenger travel is almost entirely a thing of the past, intentionally hearken to old ways. Yet even as they were written and sung at the peak of rail travel, most country train songs themselves lionized transience, not permanence, and times ahead, not those behind. These are apparently traditional and nostalgic songs themselves enamored with restless movement and progress.

✂✂✂✂✂✂

"America is the land of zero," it has been said. "Start from zero, we start from nothing. That is the idea of America."[15] One of our most prized myths is that United States was created ex nihilo, built on basically unoccupied land, that it is really and definitively a New World. If you can start from zero, there is nothing to look back to, no cultural and historical baggage to lug into the future. Thus the great American myths of innocence and progress are innately coupled and equally primordial—one cannot be scrutinized without implicating and potentially threatening the other. Perhaps this is a good part of the reason that criticisms of progress are so roundly and completely resisted in America. To see anything but glory and goodness in progress can immediately invite accusations of dubious patriotism and the entirely stigmatized status of being a Luddite. But what we need is of course not a flat and simple dismissal of progress—there are countless ways in which technological and social advance has made the modern and "progressive" era a time more inhabitable and hospitable to more people than any previous era. The problem is not that the myth of progress lacks any truth; it is that progress is not the whole truth. The uncritical embrace of progress hides or erases the actual past. And starting from an illusory past means we can only move into an illusory future. Nostalgia is not so much the honoring of living tradition, which is dynamic, as it is a mockery and carica-ture of tradition. It renders the past static and quaint. In this vein the social critic Christopher Lasch astutely scored nostalgia as the "abdi-cation of memory," making history foreign and obscuring authentic connections between the past and the present.[16]

The nostalgic and romantic account of railroading in America pro-vides an excellent case study of history largely forgotten and dis-torted, with unsavory consequences for the present and future. As we have seen, much country music promotes the train for its speed and mobility, its associations with the freedom of the individual from encumbering relationships and histories. In this regard, such recount-ing and remembering speciously bolsters the illusion of individual autonomy and self-invention. It serves a putatively conservative pol-itics that is ever keen to the dangers of big government, suspicious of governmental regulation or oversight, and looks for solutions to all difficulties or injustices in the mechanisms of the unfettered market. This leaves Americans vulnerable to the unchecked, not always inno-cent will of massive corporations, and blind to the reality that moder-nity begat two, not one, leviathans—the ever-expanding market as well as big government.

In fact, in the nineteenth century the southern and later western frontiers of the United States knew almost no settlement without its vanguard, railroad progress. And the railways in turn were not possi-ble without monumental assistance from government. In the West, it was the federal government that sent the U.S. Army ahead of the

Union Pacific, Kansas Pacific, and Northern Pacific, conducting war across the Great Plains, evacuating and subduing the Lakota, Cheyenne, and Arapaho Indians. As Solnit observes, the Plains Indians were dependent on buffalo for food, shelter, and clothing.

> The army shrewdly estimated that annihilating the buffalo would sabotage the nomadic hunting way of life of the Plains Indians and make them far easier to coerce onto reservations. [William Tecumseh] Sherman was using the same scorched-earth policy in the West than he had in the South during the Civil War. The great turning point was 1872. The Kansas Pacific Railroad was finished, and its western terminal at Dodge City became a collecting point for buffalo hides (as well as for cattle; the much-romanticized Texas cattle drives were bringing cows to railroads; the railroads were transporting them to the vast slaughterhouses of Chicago; and Chicago was reducing them to meat for national consumption: cowboys too were part of the far-reaching new economy).

The government donated massive tracts of land beneath and alongside the railways to increasingly centralized and monopolizing corporations. All told, these corporations were gifted with 204,688 square miles of line, an area a third larger than the state of California. The feds also stepped in to quell labor unrest. By the 1870s, the westward-stretching railroad giants had aroused opposition to their corruption and monopolization. The Great Strike of 1873 was a revolt against the railroads, spreading from Baltimore as far west as Kansas City, in protest of the reduction of already low wages. Soldiers were mobilized and sometimes fired into crowds to intimidate demonstrators.[17]

The role of government was similarly instrumental to railroad construction throughout the South. In Florida, the state legislature in a single year (1884) ceded 22,360,000 acres of public domain to the railroads. Over time, Texas granted to twelve railroads more than 32,000,000 acres, a territory cumulatively larger than the state of Indiana. Later many railways would doubly profit by selling granted land back to immigrants. The Southern Pacific so sold 3,000,000 acres in Texas and Louisiana during the closing years of the nineteenth century. In 1903, J. P. Morgan's Southern Railroad settled 2,000 families on 2,270,018 acres. The Louisville and Nashville

(L & N) sold 105,154 acres of farmland and 255,540 acres of timber and mining property in 1905. With land grants, tax exemptions, and loans, governments steadily assisted railroad construction and maintenance, as well as city settlement along the rail lines. In the 1870s, the Virginia legislature sold state stock holdings in railroads at a huge loss, turning nearly all over to private hands, and relieved state control and regulation. During Reconstruction, Alabama railroads received such extravagant aid that it nearly bankrupted the state. The L & N, by what historian C. Vann Woodward denotes a "process of aggression, colonization, city building, and acquisition," achieved predominance in Kentucky and ran lines to Memphis, New Orleans, Mobile, Atlanta, and Savannah. In its drive to monopolization, the L & N somehow succeeded in identifying its cause with the downtrodden, post-Civil War South, an accomplishment all the more curious since the L & N was owned by Northern and European capital—and had provided rail service to the Union Army during the war. Eventually, with monopolization and strong-arming, the railroads aroused opposition in the South as they did in the West. Milton Hannibal Smith, who operated the L & N for thirty-eight years, all too candidly confessed that he managed his lines on the theory that "society, as created, was for the purpose of one man's getting what the other fellow has, if he can, and keep out of the penitentiary." At the turn of the century, reform politicians such as Kentucky gubernatorial candidate William Goebel replaced the steamroller with the locomotive as a symbol of oppression.[18]

<hr>

Americans have always and properly been concerned about the dangers of big government. But what the history of U.S. railroading shows is how misleading it is to blame government for the ills of progress while crediting capitalism with only the benefits of progress. One of the most threatening and suffocating aspects of the modernity wrought by progress has been roundly excoriated by both the political left and the political right. I mean the breathtakingly rapid expansion of bureaucracy. Modern bureaucracy arises economically and politically when work is broken into specialized and systematized roles, then overseen by centralized authority far from the actual location of a particular work site. Administrating from afar and over vast territories and populations, bureaucracies proliferate inflexible rules, which in itself creates resentment from workers. In addition, as bureaucracy assumes a superhuman scale, it takes on a life of its own, so that even managers feel entrapped and determined by it. (What employee has not, on one or more disturbed occasions, petitioned a sympathetic manager who would like to help but says his or her hands are bureaucratically tied?) We do well to resist and lessen bureaucracy to any feasible degree. But we will never enjoy appreciable success if we remain sensitive only to government bureaucracy, while grossly overlooking and failing to name the bureaucracy of the market.

Consider the bureaucratization of our time. Before the railroads, the flow of human life was integrally connected to nature—more specifically, to the rising and setting of the sun. Noon was that approximate point when, wherever you were, the sun appeared to be highest and directly overhead. Affairs were conducted and appointments kept flexibly, not by the minute but by the quarter- or half-hour. For instance, church worship started around the middle of Sunday morning, after everyone had arrived. And on other days of the week it made no difference if you were a few minutes late for the stagecoach's appointed departure or the ship's scheduled launch. No one was keeping or marking time so precisely; the coach or the boat would wait.

This changed with the advent of the locomotive and its landscape-devouring speed. The result was the standardization of time, which is why what we now refer to as Greenwich Time was originally called Railroad Time. Before the standard time zones instituted at the behest of railroads, noon in Chicago registered on clocks in St. Louis as 11:50, as 12:17 in Toledo, and as 11:27 in Omaha. The state of Illinois had twenty-seven local times, Wisconsin thirty-eight. For a while railroads tried to operate with both local times and their own designated times, across a plethora of time zones. Each railway company had its own customized clock, so that a railroad station had as many clocks as it did separately owned lines (as well as a clock for a given station's local time). So Pittsburgh's station, for example, operated with six different time zones. All this proved confusing and infeasible, so that by 1833 the railroad companies agreed to divide the United States into four separate and standardized time zones (Atlantic, Central, Mountain, and Pacific)—long before these zones were legally and governmentally made official in 1918. In short, "In the course of the nineteenth century, time ceased to be a phenomenon that linked humans to the cosmos and became one administered by technicians to link industrial activities to one another."[19] Government bureaucratized time, but business did it first.

Likewise, the bureaucratization and standardization of goods, and their reduction to manageable and interchangeable "products," was enabled by railroads and the needs of an extended marketplace. It was one thing to buy or trade for lumber or meat with a trusted and accountable neighbor. It was another to receive such goods from a distance, from unknown origins. How can you be sure of the quality and quantity of your purchase without the slightest idea of the producer's identity, let alone integrity? Only bureaucratization will do, standardizing and measuring quality and quantity as precisely and consistently as possible. Thus even livestock must be reducible to abstractly measurable product: pigs, cows, chickens are standardized and rendered as fungible units. The logic and practical outcome is ineluctable. Much as they may sometimes resist one another, modern government and market must create and maintain bureaucracy in tandem. As Marco d'Eramo observes,

> Nothing must be left to chance. To this end, it has been established that live cattle, bought and sold in units of 40,000 pounds, must be composed of medium-sized animals, each weighing 1,050 to 1,200 pounds, with a maximum deviation of 100 pounds. In lumber [market] futures, the maximum humidity allowed per unit (11,880 ft.) is fixed at 19 percent; furthermore, the wood must be cut in rectangular planks, bound together with steel tape and paper-wrapped in batches of planks of a length no less than eight feet and no more than twenty feet, in accordance with the federal criteria for construction timber, which may come only from the states of California, Idaho, Montana, Nevada, Oregon, Washington or Wyoming. . . . The list of regulations is endless.[20]

If a preponderance of country train songs romanticize the railroads (their speed, their association with freedom and self-reinvention) and progress, there are some that acknowledge the shadow side of progress (such as bureaucratization). Easily the most famous song recognizing the alienating and dehumanizing aspects of progress is "The Legend of John Henry." It was a favorite of Cash's. He committed an eight-and-one-half-minute version of it to record on his 1963 album commemorating the working man (*Blood, Sweat, and Tears*), recorded it again on *Live at Folsom Prison*, and sang it in concerts over decades.[21]

John Henry is an African American steel driver, laying track and driving spikes with his mighty hammer, so he does not protest the presence of the railroad itself. But Henry is deeply disturbed when mechanization goes a step further and the steam drill appears to displace flesh-and-blood spike drivers. The machine is not simply putting him out of a job—it is an intrusion alien to nature, against the will of God. "Did the Lord say that machines ought to take the place of livin'?" John Henry asks. "Do engines get rewarded for their steam?" To underscore his point, Henry directly addresses the steam drill, and of course receives no reply. The heroic worker then declares that the drill "can't replace a steel-drivin' *man*" and takes the drill on in a spike-driving duel. The amazing John Henry bests the machine but kills himself doing it. Tellingly, Henry is buried near the tracks, where trains trundle by "picking up speed." Now that John Henry is dead—mute and inert—the machinery finally speaks, and the great chugging, puffing, clattering locomotive has the last word. "John Henry" originates from at least the earliest years of the twentieth century and is the most recorded ballad in American history.[22] The song's extended popularity indicates the tragic resonance it held for a long line of musicians and listeners who recognized that ways of life and vocations were lost, not simply gained, with industrial progress.

The inflexible and even death-dealing dictates of industrial bureaucracy are glimpsed in the subgenre of train wreck songs. These pieces often center on the locomotive's engineer, depicted as a heroic individual. In "Casey Jones" and "Ben Dewberry's Final Run," the train's pilots are extolled for their bravery. On "Final Run" Jimmie Rodgers repeatedly praises Dewberry as a man "without any fear."[23] Similarly, the nameless engineer of "The Wreck of the Old 97" dauntlessly pushes his locomotive to ninety miles per hour on a downhill grade and is found in the consequent wreck "with his hand on the throttle, scalded to death by the steam." In "Jones" and "Old 97," as well as "Engine 143," the doomed engineers are seen as acceptable casualties, tragic figures who courageously but helplessly take "orders" from a faceless bureaucracy. They must perilously race their trains to make up lost time and bring their cargo through on schedule, even if it kills them. In Cash's rendition of "Casey Jones," the noble pilot mounts "the cabin with his orders in his hand" and foretells his death, declaring this is "his farewell trip to that Promised Land." The unflappable Ben Dewberry checks his watch as he pushes his locomotive past its limits, shakes his head, and stoically announces to his crew, "We may make Atlanta but we'll all be dead."[24]

The thrill of reckless speed pervades many of these songs: Cash's headlong live delivery of "Old 97" on *Johnny Cash at San Quentin* is particularly rousing. And though the heroic engineers' deaths are graphically described, other fatalities are not so much as mentioned—this though Dewberry's and Jones's locomotives collide with *passenger* trains. In these regards, train wreck songs can romanticize and individualize, and so erase social dynamics, including bureaucratic responsibility for multiple fatalities.[25] That said, "Casey Jones" includes the recognition that "headaches and heartaches and all kind of pain are all a part of a railroad train." And if Cash's rendition of "Old 97" thrills, making the wreck the train-age equivalent of ever larger and more astonishing cinematic explosions, his performance of "Engine 143" is starkly different. Here the tempo is slowed nearly to a dirge, and throbbing electric instrumentation is replaced by plaintive acoustic guitar. Cash vocalizes with a doleful echo. The engineer receives "*strict* orders" to make up time and, most remarkably, is said to have been "*murdered* upon a railroad."[26] Thus his death is not merely accidental and implacable; bureaucrats, though unnamed, are assigned homicidal culpability. Social dynamics and responsibility are here not totally elided.

That said, country music historian Bill Malone is surely correct that country music largely reflects a deep and often blinding individualism. That individualism is "the belief that if there's a solution to be found, it's going to be found through individual exertion. And if it can't be found, then you just fatally accept it, or flee from it—flee into fantasy or into religion or into the bottle or into geographic movement. If you're not satisfied here, go someplace else, or retreat into anger, violence—all kinds of individual responses outside of collective action."[27] Country music is thus not consistently socially aware.

In the North and the nation's most populous cities, the railroads bound metropolitan areas into increasingly dense webs: factories and subsequently populations of factory workers concentrated near railhead shipping points. In the agrarian and more scarcely populated South, the nineteenth-century railroads had the opposite effect. They "overwhelmingly connected [rural] areas of rich agricultural production with [distant urban] centers of export."[28] Rural southerners were well aware that the railroads—and the timber and mining industries enabled by them—were carrying the riches of the land away to far-removed cities, leaving those who lived and toiled on the land with nothing more than inadequate wages. But, true to its typical individualization, country music rarely names this colonization of rural America by urban America or the domination of labor's have-nots by capital's haves. Indeed, this may mark the single clearest distinction between what is labeled "folk music" and what is designated "country music." After all, instrumentation, attention to the common people, nasally and twangy vocalization, and much of the songbooks are identical in the two musics. But if country music is marked and bounded by individualism, folk music is ready to mobilize and rabble-rouse, and certainly to conceive of social action and social responsibility. Thus Sarah Ogan Gunning's "Coalminers" (1937) boldly beckons miners, who "work and slave for a dollar in the company store," to wake up: "Open your eyes and see what this dirty capitalistic system has done to you and me."[29] Folk artists Jean Ritchie, in her "The L & N Don't Stop Here Anymore," and John Prine, with his "Paradise," call attention to the ravages of progress, to landscapes destroyed and rusting towns depleted and left for dead. Prine's lyrics are especially pointed. His song's narrator asks his father to return him to his hometown of Paradise, in Muhlenberg County, Kentucky. The father informs his son that there is no Paradise to return to: "Mr. Peabody's coal train has hauled it away." Prine's narrator acutely observes that the coal company's shovels stripped forests and left the land forsaken, then attributed it all to "the progress of man."[30]

It is a testimony to Johnny Cash's courage, historical sensitivity, and refusal to honor dubious lines between "country" and "folk" music that he recorded covers of both "L & N" and "Paradise."

Taking the measure of the American enthrallment to modern progress, Christopher Lasch lamented that both the political left and the political right refuse to countenance talk about scientific, technological, and practical limits. Both hold to a "belief in the desirability and inevitability of technical and economic development." We might think that conservatives would be skeptical of unbounded progress, but American conservatism's "ritual deference to 'traditional values' cannot hide the right's commitment to progress, unlimited economic growth, and acquisitive individualism." Indeed, it is the right that has most stubbornly resisted the development of sustainable energy and downplayed or denied the reality of global warning. Today, Lasch's urgent words from 1991 appear all the more prescient.

> The right proposes, in effect, to maintain our riotous standard of living, as it has been maintained in the past, at the expense of the rest of the world (increasingly at the expense of our own minorities as well). This program is self-defeating, not only because it will produce environmental effects from which even the rich cannot escape but because it will widen the gap between the rich and poor nations, generate more and more violent movements of insurrection and terrorism against the West, and bring about the deterioration of the world's political climate as threatening as the deterioration of its physical climate.

Meanwhile, the left's historical program of extending Western progress and standards of living to the entire world "has become equally self-defeating" and will "lead even more quickly to the exhaustion of nonrenewable resources" and ecological catastrophe.[31]

The profound ideological enthrallment to progress, spanning America's entire political spectrum, makes the church's division and side-taking in pitched "red vs. blue" culture wars all the more futile and depressing. Yet if there is little room for the facile American resort to "optimism" (itself a dogma of the religion of progress), there remains capacious space for something sturdier and more profound: hope. The Christian church still holds in its tradition promising treasures and resources to step outside the crippled and constrained terms of debate fostered by the cult of progress.

First of all, the church is gifted with the theological vocabulary and conceptuality to name untrammeled and unquestionable progress for what it is—idolatry and the usurpation of prerogatives Scripture and tradition assign only to God. Made a religion, progress is that faith that takes humanity as "the measure of all things" and preaches that human ingenuity can build heaven on earth. The Christian church has a different confession: that unaided humanity cannot save itself, that only the work of the creating and redeeming God can rescue creation and bring it to maturity and perfection. As the brilliantly aphoristic G. K. Chesterton recognized, those in thrall to the cult of progress are enslaved by a faith more "crushing" and dictatorial than that of any traditional pietist.

> They are not allowed to question that whatever has recently happened was all for the best. Now Progress is Providence without God. That is, it is a theory that everything has always perpetually gone right by accident. It is a sort of atheistic optimism, based on an everlasting coincidence far more miraculous than a miracle. If there be no purpose, or if the purpose permits of human free will, then in either case it is almost insanely unlikely that there should be in history a period of steady and uninterrupted progress; or in other words a period in which poor bewildered humanity moves amid a chaos of complications, without making a single mistake. What has to be hammered into the head of most normal newspaper-readers to-day is that Man has made a great many mistakes, Modern Man has made a great many mistakes.[32]

In its most basic convictions, then, and in its constitutive practice of worshiping the living God of Israel and Jesus Christ, the church is granted vision to name cultic progress as a destructive idolatry. Not buying the illusion that whatever has most recently happened, or has now come under the purview of technological manipulation, is nec-

essarily for the best, the church provides a vantage point to question
and critique "the latest advance." It is a vantage point from which to
work at discernment of whether or not this particular development is
truly an advance and entirely a good. Put concisely, the church
through its faith has the imaginative resources to discern and count
the costs of progress as well as its gains.[33]

In addition, the Christian church taking stock of its legacy can recognize in the religion of progress a manifestation of one of the oldest
heresies it has battled—the heresy of Gnosticism. Various as they
were, the earliest gnostics tended to denigrate material, physical creation and ultimately sought escape from the body and natural creation
through a disembodied intellectual and spiritual knowledge (*gnosis*).
Dismissive of the material and physical, Gnosticism sees the body as
dispensable or at best instrumental—it may be used or manipulated
at the pleasure of its "owner." As a kind of Gnosticism, modern
progress now sees nothing less than the human genome as its laboratory. It also takes little note of concrete places and specific locales—
food, minerals, clothing, and other bounties of creation appear in
endless supply, and as if from nowhere. Practical Gnosticism, a lux-
ury of the affluent, remains blithely and steadfastly unaware of the
ravages of capitalistic globalization in distant, unknown communities. A church aware of its tradition and the pitfalls of Gnosticism in
the guise of progress cannot remain so blind.

Finally, the Christian church through its treasures of life and practice possesses the potential to claim and be claimed by a living tradition. As Lasch suggested, much of the current clamor for "tradition"
and "traditional values" rings shallow and untrue. It is too often a vain
and ritualistic deference, mock bowing to mere shells or pale ghosts
of any actual tradition. It holds up a nostalgic and faux traditionalism
as a power play to exclude or suppress the marginalized, to contain
developments threatening to vested interests. This is nowhere more
nakedly evident than in the refusal of so many of today's "conservatives" and "traditionalists" to take account of how much consumer
capitalism contributes to so many of the ills they decry. For instance,
strengths of character, stability, and commitment are undermined by
the consumer capitalistic ethos. The addiction to novelty and
"planned obsolescence" has overtaken not only formerly durable

consumer goods, but relationships such as marriage and loyal friendship. Consumer capitalism thrives on moral and social permissiveness, commodifying and endlessly profiting from its successful promotion of ever more choice in every realm of human experience. Nothing is sacred in the sense of being pricelessly beyond the grasp of the market.[34]

The church (to say nothing of the great Jewish faith preceding and birthing it) has not survived for 2,000 years without the development of something more than a static, utterly unchangeable, and merely exploitable tradition. Participating in a genuinely organic, dynamic tradition, the church draws on the present as well as past: it is not a museum piece under glass so much as an ongoing, "socially embodied argument."[35] In more concrete terms, the living Christian tradition is the bridge between the past and the future. Thus tradition in the present tense—the living, developing bridge between past and future—is always changing. As George Orwell noted, "Nothing ever stands still. We must add to our heritage or lose it, we must grow greater or grow less, we must go forward or go backward."[36]

In this vein, Christian tradition and the communion of the saints is the "democracy of the dead,"[37] looking to the past for a valuable vantage point outside imprisonment to the present—not for dictatorial mandates to be merely mimicked in today's world, but for indispensable perspective and counsel on the hazards facing, now and tomorrow, those coming after the many faithful who have gone before us. The church as just such a living tradition stands for progress, yes, but not at any cost—and certainly not at the cost of God's good creation and humanity's very soul.

Chapter 5

Guilt and Innocence

*J*ack Cash died for less than three dollars. That was the day's wage Johnny's older brother was earning for cutting fence posts over a table saw on May 12, 1944. Johnny (or J.R., as the family then knew him) tried to persuade his brother to go fishing with him, but Jack said the family needed money and went to work. Feeding wood into the saw, the 14-year-old somehow got entangled and pulled into the spinning round blade. It split Jack open from his rib cage to his groin. He would live eight days after the accident. He succumbed on a Sunday, seeing heavenly visions and hearing angelic song.

Jack was tall and strong. He was little brother J.R.'s protector, role model, and guide. In terms of constancy and responsibility, he may have been more the man of the family than their father, who was often drunk and explosive. On that spring day in 1944, J.R. was walking back from the fishing hole when his father, Ray, appeared in a car driven by a preacher. In the description of one biographer, Ray Cash was "a stump of a man whose face forever seemed on the brink of rage or tears."[1] At this moment Ray's face was near tears. He told his son to throw his pole in the ditch and get in the car, that something terrible had happened. When the preacher dropped them off, Ray directed Johnny to the smokehouse near the family's home. Inside, under the hanging meat and amid the smell of curing bacon, Mr. Cash picked up a bag and dumped out a ruined shirt and khaki pants, soaking in blood. Jack's belt, sliced in two, also tumbled out. Upon showing his youngest son these bloody clothes, Ray Cash told the boy what had happened and that their beloved Jack would probably die.

At the time J.R. Cash was twelve years old, the age of account-ability in the Baptist tradition in which he was reared. Twelve is when a Baptist can be baptized as an adult.

Why did Ray Cash show a barely adolescent boy his mortally injured brother's torn and soiled clothes? The accounts are murky. There was a precedent, of a kind. Ray's own father died when Ray was a child, and Ray was raised by his older brother, Dave. Once Dave took young Ray to a forced viewing of the burned, hanging body of a black man Dave had helped lynch. Ray was horrified, but stood quietly under the tree, looking up at the corpse. "You didn't say anything to Dave," he said years later. "If you didn't like it, you just kept your mouth shut."[2]

Did Ray, who admitted his own "weird raising," think this is how you fathered a boy in the face of violent death? That you toughened him by making him stare directly at it, or at least at its horrible effects? Or (and?) did the elder Cash hold J.R. responsible for Jack's death? Only many years later could the grown-up Johnny Cash admit that his father, at least once, in an alcoholic outburst, told him that he should have died rather than the saintly Jack, who went to work for the family while J.R. was gone fishing.

In any event, the 12-year-old J.R. experienced the incident as supersaturated with guilt. The morning after the accident, he and his mother went to visit Jack. The mortally injured boy spoke to his mother but said nothing to his little brother. "And as the years went by, that was one thing I never could understand," Johnny Cash said decades afterward. "Why Jack didn't look at me, and why he didn't have anything to say to me . . ."[3] The incident and its memory were so charged that Cash on some level could even recall Jack's death as not accidental, but a homicide. In 1995, he told an interviewer that, though nothing could be proved and his parents never had called it murder, "I always thought of it as murder."[4] Speaking when he was in his sixties, Cash said Jack still appeared in his dreams every couple of months, the elder sibling as superego or conscience personi-fied. Jack is mature, always two years older than Johnny's current age. He is the ordained minister he hoped to be when he grew up. "Usually in my Jack dreams I'm having some sort of problem or I'm doing something questionable, and I'll notice him looking at me, smiling, as if to say, 'I know you, J.R. I know what you've *really* got in your mind . . .' There's no fooling Jack."[5]

In some ways, J.R. Cash's experience of Jack's death made Johnny Cash. His friends noticed that he turned introspective and pensive. He began writing stories and poems. He became aware of his mortality. He discovered a sense of his own imperfection and could identify with the convict, the despised, the outsider. He never again thought of himself as innocent. You might just as well tell the truth about inner darkness to yourself and to others. "There's no fooling Jack."

❆❆❆❆❆❆❆

On this count of no pretense to innocence, Johnny Cash was quintessentially un-American. America as a nation has always considered itself unique and exceptional. It is the place where the world got a chance to start over, to be born again into a new innocence. The myth of American innocence only intensified in the twentieth century. President Woodrow Wilson insisted that the United States had "no selfish ends to serve" on its entrance into World War I. European nations fought the war for conquest or material compensation or revenge, but America battled for nothing more or less than "the ultimate peace of the world."[6] The myth of magnificent innocence was bolstered by Wilsonian accounts of World War II—America enters another sordid European conflict, taking up arms reluctantly but bravely and with unprecedented effectiveness, and rids the world of the demonic evil of Nazism. More recently, as the political scientist (and Vietnam War veteran) Andrew Bacevich writes, "Our own day has seen the revival of Wilsonian ambitions and Wilsonian certainty, this time, however, combining with a pronounced affinity for the sword." In the 1980s, "Wilson's truest disciple," Ronald Reagan, reasserted the United States' "power to begin the world over again." Bill Clinton declared the United States on the "right side of history." And George W. Bush, heralded by admirers as "the most Wilsonian president since Wilson himself," took America's innocence and correlative salvific powers to extreme lengths, appropriating for America the role Scripture assigns to Jesus Christ, as "the light that shines in the darkness, and the darkness will not overcome it" (John 1:5).[7] True to the account of American innocence, this nation can rid the world of evil, act as a benevolent empire, wield (and deploy) nuclear and other military capabilities no other nation can be entrusted with, and, like Almighty God the Judge of the Universe, launch Operation Infinite Justice. The Founding Fathers actually worried about the concentration of power, even in American hands, but we now witness the illusion of American innocence taken to its most fantastic lengths ever.

The myth of such absolute innocence, with its accompanying entitlements of unchecked power, can be sustained only with strenuous, repressive denial and intentional ignorance of history. America as the Savior Angel of humanity is but the mirror image of the equally incredible designation of America as the Great Satan. Among other things, maturity is the capacity to understand that one is not the center of the universe (or even of Mother's entire attention). Maturity means the assumption of appropriate responsibility, the ability and willingness to take credit where credit is due and blame where blame is due. It means admitting, not denying, our actions and their consequences—then acting accordingly. The United States is without doubt a great actor in and on world history, but nothing holds it back from becoming a democracy for grown-ups so much as the myth of innocence. As Cornel West observes, "We are exceptional because of our denial of the antidemocratic foundation stones of American democracy. No other democratic nation revels so blatantly in such self-deceptive innocence, such self-paralyzing reluctance to confront the nightmare of its own history. This sentimental flight from history—or adolescent escape from painful truths about ourselves—means that even as we grow old, grow big, and grow powerful, we have yet to grow up."[8]

American innocence, with its plenitude of dangerous and infantilizing effects, can be maintained only by forgetting American history from its very inception. There was no golden age of absolute innocence; slavery and racism cannot be recognized as minor (and so now negligible) subplots in the American story. African Americans, slaves in the land of the free, incarnated America's deepest contradiction.[9] Most of the Old South did not simply contain slavery as a feature, but was a society constituted by slavery, based on slave labor.[10] Northern attitudes and institutions (themselves hardly pure of racism) unfolded largely in response—whether endorsing or aversive—to southern realities. The race issue stands as a central if not the sole cause of the Civil War, which, as we have seen, was in many ways not entirely lost by the South. So many things are the way they now are because of the way they were. The nihilistic despair of much of black urban America; the matriarchalism of African American culture; the resilience and defiance of popular culture; the glories and sorrows of African American Christianity; the (literal) complexion of American sports—these and many other realities cannot be understood or appreciated even slightly without a careful memory of slavery and the ongoing degradation of black Americans subsequent to slavery.[11] Yet the willful determination to forget or ignore the history of American racism crops up ever anew. Thus, incredibly, mainstream American leadership and media regarded O. J. Simpson's acquittal as a sudden revelation that the nation's judicial system is broken, as if judges and juries before then had constantly been fair to all defendants, including blacks. Even more absurdly, 9/11 is routinely represented as the first large-scale occurrence of terrorism on American soil, as if the Ku Klux Klan had never existed and pogroms had never destroyed black communities from Tulsa, Oklahoma, to Springfield, Illinois.[12]

※※※※※※

The speciousness and costs of American innocence come clear in any honest recall of our history, but they are perhaps especially illumined from a theological angle. Christians in particular should be deeply skeptical of the myth of innocence, because it denies the classical doctrine of original sin. This doctrine holds that all of humanity, collectively and individually, is mired in sin. This sinfulness entails that no human vision of the right and the good is entirely unclouded, no human action completely pure. All persons, even the most virtuous, are susceptible to self-deception and the corruptions of power. Furthermore, because of original sin, neither humanity nor any part of humanity can save or perfect itself. Ultimate redemption and justice cannot be achieved or managed by human ability—it rests finally and only in the hands of God. So American exceptionalism and innocence are insupportable from a biblical and Christian understanding of human nature. On the other hand, the checks and balances arrangement of American democracy—guarding against concentrated and unaccountable power in any wing or agency of government—is one of its most profoundly Christian intuitions. A democracy inflected by this Christian reading of the human and political predicament, crystallized through the insights of Augustine, is not based on any presumption of innocence and human goodness. Instead, it is premised "precisely upon the permanent presence of imperfect humans who must, by dint of their equal insufficiency and the permanency of need, inhabit, and govern together, cities of men."[13]

The myth of American innocence, then, denies original sin and cuts off at the knees a classical Christian warrant for the legitimacy of democratic governance. The myth is a seedbed for a distinctly unchristian triumphalism, the expectation that if only the right people or right nation can attain power, then that power will, by definition, be used benevolently. Accordingly, Jesus Christ is rendered as the ally of the powerful, the divine-human supporter of the status quo, the great endorser of righteous empire. In recent decades, an impressive spectrum of biblical scholars and theologians has renewed focus on the obvious: ancient Israel was only very briefly any kind of empire, and that imperial moment was not only brief but less than shining. Otherwise, from exodus to exile, Israel struggled to survive as the people of God under a succession of oppressive empires, from Egypt to Rome. The biblical God was constantly concerned for the slave, the stranger, the widowed and the orphaned, the destitute and the disregarded. For the Hebrew prophets especially, the God Israel encountered was one who, in the words of a venerable African American prayer, "sits high and looks low."[14]

It is no accident that, decades before European and Anglo American biblical scholars would emphasize as much, Christian black Americans remembered Jesus was a Jew. In a classic published in 1949, the great African American churchman Howard Thurman argued that a proper account of Jesus of Nazareth began with the "simple historical fact" that he was a "poor Jew." As such, Jesus was "a member of a minority group [first-century Palestinian Israel] in the midst of a larger dominant and controlling group [imperial Rome]." This Jesus, the Jesus of the Gospels, founded a faith community that would learn and practice after him "a technique of survival for the oppressed." Recognizing this Jesus, Thurman warned, in words all too pertinent for twenty-first-century imperial America:

> Too often the price exacted by society for security and respectability is that the Christian movement in its formal expression must be on the side of the strong against the weak. This is a matter of tremendous significance, for it reveals to what extent a religion that was born of a people acquainted with persecution and suffering has become the cornerstone of a civilization and of nations whose very position in modern life has too often been secured by a ruthless use of power applied to weak and defenseless people.[15]

Triumphalism and the myth of innocence make for a volatile mix. Triumphalism arrogates power beyond accountability and is all too easily open to abuse. The myth of innocence, meanwhile, represses any acknowledgment of abuse and its subsequent guilt.

In an intriguing passage in his *The Mind of the South,* W. J. Cash suggests that the southern cult and adoration of white womanhood brewed in the cauldron of slavery, dehumanizing to masters as well as slaves. Slavery was a brutally coercive institution, with the lash always at its core. The whip-wielding master found in himself a bestial sadism he would rather not have known or seen. In addition, masters often took advantage of female slaves, whom they regarded as more "natural" and sensual than their cultivated, idealized wives. Rather than confront the resultant guilt and admit that his way of life was decidedly not innocent, the brutalizing and brutalized master intuited that "the [betrayed white] woman must be compensated, the revolting suspicion in the male that he might be slipping into bestiality got rid of, by glorifying her; the Yankee must be answered by proclaiming from the housetops that Southern Virtue, so far from being inferior, was superior, not alone to the North's but to any on earth, and adducing Southern Womanhood in proof." As an example of what he refers to as "gyneolatry," Cash records a popular toast in Georgia of the 1830s: "Woman! The center and circumference, diameter and periphery, sine, tangent and secant of all our affections."[16] (Gyneolators or not, this toast was apparently formulated by passionate adepts of geometry.) Cash's analysis sheds light not only on the cult of southern womanhood, but on the countless twentieth-century cases when lynching and other racial attacks were preceded by allegations that a black male had sexually accosted a white female. Here the supreme symbol of white virtue and innocence—itself tellingly fragile and vulnerable in a setting patriarchal as well as racist—is threatened by the black avatar of master-class guilt and the very object that, if kept impotent, secured a sense of white superiority among males.

The tendency to scapegoating, while of course not unique to America, shows up repeatedly and in many guises through American history. The ironies proliferate pell-mell. Consider the popular genre of the western, which peaked on television in 1959. In that year no fewer than twenty-six programs were horse operas. In the eyes of conservative evangelicals such as James Dobson and Jerry Falwell, the 1950s epitomize America's halcyon age, before the country tumbled into the dark libertinism of the 1960s and 1970s. In 1987, when Pat Robertson launched The Family Channel, he loaded its schedule with westerns from the late fifties and early sixties.[17] The series of this vintage were thought to be sterling standards of family values. Yet it is almost impossible to find an intact mother-father-children nuclear family in the lot.[18] Consider *The Gene Autry Show* (1950–56), whose star is known for kissing only his horse, Champion, and can never hold down a job—from week to week Gene is variously a rancher, a cowhand, a sheriff, a border agent, and so on. Many of the TV western heroes—not just Gene Autry, but Marshal Dillon on *Gunsmoke* (1955–75) and the titular characters on *The Lone Ranger* (1949–57) and *The Virginian* (1962–71)—are confirmed bachelors. Others are not only bachelors but desultory gamblers and con artists (the brothers and cousins on *Maverick* [1957–62], Paladin on *Have Gun, Will Travel* [1957–63], the lead on *Bat Masterson* [1958–61]). In the few outstanding instances where parents and their offspring actually are together, the families are headed by widows or widowers. Lucas McCain on *Rifleman* (1958–63) rears his young son alone. On *The Big Valley* (1965–69), Barbara Stanwyck regally plays a matriarch over her brood of four adult children: two sons and a daughter, all born of herself and her late husband—and the illegitimate son of the same late husband, now welcomed into the fold by his stepmother and half-brothers and sister. Meanwhile, over at the Ponderosa, on the long-running *Bonanza* (1959–73), Ben Cartwright ranches and dispenses free-lance justice with his three grown sons, each birthed by a separate and deceased wife. Both of the latter two shows feature a running gag: on occasion a Cartwright scion or one of *The Big Valley*'s Barkley clan will fall in love and even get married, but in that same episode the new spouse will be killed off or otherwise meet an anguished death.

All genres have their conventions. Why has the western so resolutely centered on singles or broken families? Surely it has much to do with our typical conception of life in the Old West—dangerous, physically demanding, crude: no place for women and children. But I suspect it also to do with the myth of American innocence. The West's macho mythos of violence, combined with that of innocence, demanded scapegoats, albeit often noble ones.

Two cinematic representatives suffice to display the type, which recurs again and again in westerns. In *Shane* (1953), the hero is a lonely gunfighter who happens on to a farmer, his wife, and young son, and hires on as a hand. It is an idyllic existence for our hero; he is, within the bosom of a family, contented and steadily freed of his demons. But the idyll cannot last, not for Shane. Blatant evil, in the form of several violent criminals, intrudes, and paradise can be saved only if Shane again straps on his guns. In the film's climactic scene, a thrilling shootout, he vanquishes evil. But having killed and bloodstained his hands in paradise, however necessarily, he cannot remain there. In the closing scene Shane rides off into the horizon, stoically refusing the boy's heartbreaking calls for him to return. Shane is the heroic scapegoat, whose atonement with society comes only with his voluntary exile.[19]

Our other specimen is John Ford's masterpiece, *The Searchers* (1956), which features what is widely regarded as John Wayne's greatest performance.[20] Wayne portrays Ethan Edwards, a veteran of the Confederacy returned to the Texas bosom of his brother's large family. Of course, he will not be allowed to settle down. Marauding

Indians attack and slaughter most of the family. An exception is Ethan's niece, who is kidnapped by the Indians. Ethan makes it his mission—consuming several years; his character's hair goes gray in the course of the story—to track down and rescue the niece. *The Searchers* is more self-conscious and self-critical of its root myths than earlier westerns. Ethan is clearly seen as a bigot, shooting a dead Indian in the eyes for sheer spite and otherwise regarding Indians as subhuman. In the end, he gets no "sweet revenge." When he finally locates his niece, she is now grown and wholly enculturated with the Indians, and does not want to leave with him. Nonetheless, Ethan forcibly returns her to what is left of her (white) home. He has fulfilled his mission, but, like Shane, he is impure in his bloodletting and cannot remain among the reunited family. In the film's famous closing scene, the relatives retreat into their house, while Ethan remains outside, alone. He is stunningly photographed from inside the home, framed in the doorway, the barren western vista looming hugely behind him. As dust picks up, he turns his back on the threshold of the hearth and walks into the emptiness, "bearing all their guilt away into some desolate place" (Lev. 16:22, NJB).

The TV westerns are rarely as smart or as truthful as *The Searchers*—their sanitization is what makes them safe, "family" viewing—but obviously they operate in the same diegetic universe. America's embrace of individualism, ever starting anew, and the myths of both innocence and redemptive violence, mean that the hero in the western—less popular today than before but still one of our nation's hallmark genres—cannot be the steady, committed "family man." He must instead be unattached, "free," quietly accepting of his lonely fate, so that any moment he can effect a violent purge and then carry the guilt away from united and still innocent families and communities. Thus, as Garry Wills puts it, "The archetypal American is a displaced person—arrived from a rejected past, breaking into a glorious future, on the move, fearless himself, feared by others, a killer but cleansing the world of things that 'need killing,' loving but not bound down by love, rootless but carrying the Center in himself."[21]

❊❊❊❊❊❊❊

If the classic western bares the inner workings of the machinery of the myth of American innocence, it does not expose the most insidious outworkings of this myth. After all, the western hero has chosen his destiny, is admired even as he is cast out, and will be honored in memory. Other, "real life," American scapegoats do not choose to act as scapegoats and are humiliated and despised both immediately and in remembrance. This is the case with African Americans who have been lynched and otherwise terrorized. And the innocence machinery keeps grinding away, pulling in new victims. The currently most liable scapegoat is the homosexual.

I am not dismissive of all arguments wary of endorsing homosexual behavior and identity. No respecter of tradition can toss away without a thought particular traditions that are thousands of years old. There are honest and not simply homophobic arguments made by some on behalf of the tradition as it has long stood on same-sex behavior. That patently acknowledged, the actions of too many on the religious and "traditional" right are bald attempts at scapegoating a vulnerable portion of the American population. This motivation betrays itself in disproportionate, even histrionic allegations. Sober estimates put the percentage of Americans homosexually oriented at two to five percent; the highest estimates have been at ten percent. Yet some cry that this small population will destroy the traditional family or even Western civilization. (In the most notorious case, Jerry Falwell and Pat Robertson blamed the 9/11 attacks on homosexuals, among others.)

George W. Bush's administration at first officially expressed moral concerns about homosexuality, but did not exploit it as a scapegoating "wedge" issue. Vice President Dick Cheney continued a close relationship with his openly lesbian daughter (who served on her father's presidential campaign team and declared that the legality of same-sex unions was a matter appropriately left to state, not federal, government). Bush himself approved a gay congressman for a speaking slot at his first nominating convention and directed his subordinates to make sure the Republican platform did *not* include planks opposing gay marriage (though social conservatives were finally successful in restoring the planks). Once elected, Bush became the first Republican president to appoint openly gay people to several posts in his administration. All this, of course, changed

after 9/11 and the inception of the politics of fear the Bush administration was, for years, so successful at exploiting. A Republican poll-
ster's memo in 2003 identified antigay marriage measures as "an
ideal wedge issue." It vigorously voiced opposition to gay unions
and solidified the support of conservative evangelicals—as it turns
out, Bush's most dependable base. It could also serve to split the
black vote, otherwise overwhelmingly going to Democrats. (Support
for gay marriage is lower among African Americans than any other
racial grouping.)[22]

Given all the historic and present-day pressures bearing down on
the family's stability and challenging Western civilization, it is absurd
to shift primary attention to what is demonstrably a side issue, however controversial. Such actions can be explained only by the venerable practice of scapegoating. They serve to take the majority's eye
off more profound but more generally disturbing concerns, and maintain confidence in our precious innocence. Surely I and my family
have nothing to do with family problems, even those our family suffers. And Osama Bin Laden *said* he attacked our nation because of its
policies in Iraq, Israel, and Saudi Arabia; but, since we are fundamentally innocent, he *really* hates us because we are free and good.
And/or because we are too tolerant or permissive about such things
as homosexuality. Scapegoating allows the many to pretend that
forces tearing us apart are not *among us*. It turns scrutiny outward,
most easily and alluringly onto one or more minorities.

Scapegoating thus diverts and obscures the honest and sometimes
self-critical discussion a democracy for grown-ups demands. For
Christians, it is even more fundamentally objectionable. Scapegoating implicitly denies the doctrine of original sin. More importantly, it
challenges the core Christian conviction that Jesus Christ died once
for all, for the sins of all humanity. If Jesus lived and died redemp-
tively, and victoriously rose from the grave, the sublimating sacrifice
of the vulnerable minority has ended. There cannot be any more
scapegoats. Those who scapegoat, no matter how piously they otherwise talk or behave, act as if the resurrection were a lie and Jesus
Christ died in vain.[23]

❈❈❈❈❈❈❈

In acknowledging original sin, human impotence in saving ourselves, and the human (and very American) tendency toward scapegoating, I do not intend to idealize guilt. Guiltiness is not a condition to be desired or sought after. The state of guiltiness is, to say the least, uncomfortable, and it can be destructive—especially when it is overly scrupulous and liable to false assignment. ("Blaming the victim" is one instance of such falsely assigned guilt.) Theologically considered, the state or condition we are constructively called to is responsibility. This responsibility is inherently relational: God speaks or God acts, God's creatures respond. Given not only our creaturely finitude, but the reality of our sinfulness, we sometimes respond to God's precedents poorly, maliciously, or not at all. Hence (true) guilt is a consequence of a faulty human response to God's covenanting with us.

The sociologist Philip Rieff puts it succinctly. Guilt is a "main mechanism" in a "covenanted culture" of people who are called by God but respond wrongly. "A covenanted culture," as Rieff writes, "cannot exist apart from a sense of guilt, for the most obvious fact of experience is the difficulty it presents in keeping the covenant—more important, the temptations it presents not to keep it." In our fallenness, there is something about us that urges us to chafe against our creatureliness and grateful guidance by God's covenant. We often and perversely resist the terms of the covenant. In these circumstances, it is a grace that we sense and become aware of a condition of guilt, since guilt reminds us of the covenant and its basic, loving goodness. So, says Rieff, guilt is a "ruling emotion" of every community of faith; "those inside such a culture are compelled to *responsibility for themselves.*"[24]

Exactly. Guilt compels us to responsibility for ourselves, to God. Guilt accordingly keeps us in relationship to God—it sustains us as responsible creatures when we break the covenant, when we act misguidedly or wickedly. The church or other faith community unable or unwilling to acknowledge its own guilt is irresponsible and, as such, immature. Something similar or analogous holds for a democratic people. Inasmuch as democracy is rule of the people by the people, and so long as it can endure, the people must act responsibly for themselves and for the common good. If they do not, democracy will degenerate toward anarchy and be tempted to accept the strong-arming, compulsory leadership of an authoritarian or even dictatorial regime. In Rieff's words, "[O]nly a self-critical democracy of the guilty is truly democratic."[25]

In this light, Johnny Cash's guilt over the death of his brother Jack was false guilt. Young J.R.'s presence at the lumber mill rather than the fishing hole would have made no difference. Nevertheless, the episode grew him up, primed his creative sensibilities, and caused him to know intensely the possibility of guilt—real as well as false.[26] Because he could not imagine himself as an innocent, Cash could emphathize with the outcast and the guilty (truly or falsely convicted). To listen to his live prison albums (*Folsom Prison* and *San Quentin*) is to hear a performer identifying with the prisoners, even setting himself with them against prison authorities. Referring to *Folsom,* Cash once commented that there "me and the convicts [got along] just as fellow rebels, outsiders, and miscreants should."[27] Certainly Cash could play off his rebel image; it was central to his comeback during the American Records era. But his identification with the lowly and despised was not mere posturing. In 1982, as noted earlier in these pages, Cash and his family were terrorized by armed robbers at their home in Jamaica. Well known for his advocacy of prison reform and sympathy for criminals, Cash was asked afterward what he thought about the young men who had violated his home. "I'm out of answers," he confessed. "My only certainties are that I grieve for desperate young men and the societies that produce and suffer so many of them, and I felt that I knew those boys. We had a kinship, they and I: I knew how they thought, I knew how they needed. They were like me."[28]

Some believe racism about African Americans may have stretched Cash's empathy to its limits. Though he recorded songs on the behalf of prisoners, the working man, and (as we will see) Native Americans, his music never confronted bigotry toward African Americans. More tellingly, when newspaper photos of his first wife, Vivian, appeared in 1965, and some racist groups mistook the Italian American woman as a light-skinned black, Cash feared for his record and concert sales in the South. He vigorously protested that Vivian was not African American. In doing so, he appeared implicitly to confirm the attitude that interracial marriage was repulsive. Of course, this may say more about Cash's early-sixties country-music audience than about him. He was never accused of acting with bigotry himself, and when in the late sixties and early seventies he achieved a larger and more varied fan base, he used *The Johnny Cash Show,* airing nationwide on ABC, to stare down racism against African Americans. His first episode featured the (black) R & B singer O. C. Smith. Black guest stars on later episodes included Joe Tex, and when Ray Charles appeared, Cash sat next to him on Charles's piano bench. Biographer Michael Streissguth observes, "It hardly seems radical from the vantage point of thirty years later, but [in 1970] a white man and a black man sharing a bench in some Southern towns might have found themselves on the run."[29]

In all events, Cash explicitly understood his "kinship" with the disinherited in light of his Christian convictions. Criticized for playing Vegas as well as prisons, he simply responded that "the Pharisees said the same thing about Jesus: 'He dines with publicans and sinners.' "[30] In his partisanship for the underdog, Cash was never so fiercely eloquent as when he spoke and sang out on the plight of the Native American. The dogma of North America as an unoccupied, untouched virgin wilderness is only two or three centuries old, and increasingly archaeology and other scientific and historical investigation have proved it illusory and untenable. As one historian writes of sixteenth-century Spanish explorations in the area of today's near southwest United States, these European visitors were surrounded on all sides by "the very numerous and very diverse native people," and spent "virtually every night" of their "wilderness" sojourn in a town.[31]

The story of the Native American, alongside that of the African American, is the other major historical narrative that falsifies the myth of American innocence at its roots. Cities visited by the explorer Coronado numbered as many as 100,000 in population. "From Alaska to Tierra del Fuego there were probably close to 100 million people at contact, one-sixth of the world's population."[32] What's more, these earlier inhabitants of the Americas were not simply passive pawns of nature—brutely "uncivilized" in the terms of modern progressivism. They cut trees, drained swamps, engineered water diversion systems, and built roads. They employed fire as a technology to trap deer and buffalo, drive lizards and other edibles into the open, and lessen mosquito populations.

What largely though not entirely depopulated the American continents were the European interlopers, who not only lethally claimed property but (more significantly, and basically unwittingly) introduced with themselves and their livestock waves of ravaging diseases that decimated entire Native American communities. Scientists in the first half of the twentieth century, and explorers and naturalists before, erroneously took their readings of earlier inhabitation from the ragged scraps of civilizations shredded by conquest and catastrophic disease. As one commentator puts it, "It was as if [they] had come across refugees from a Nazi prison camp, and concluded that they belonged to a culture that had always been barefoot and starving."[33]

When Johnny Cash released *Bitter Tears: Ballads of the American Indian* in 1964, the grim extent of this history was not known.[34] But more than enough was known irrefutably to evidence a string of betrayals and broken promises that marked the vanquishing of the Indian tribes across the United States and from the nation's very beginnings. On a terse and utterly stunning eight-song album, Cash occupies the narrative voices of these rundown races and unsparingly tells the story of how, from the Indian perspective, the West was lost. The album was written largely by Cash, with assists from Johnny Horton and the Pima Indian activist Peter LaFarge. The instrumentation is spartan, with some Indian drums and the guitars of Cash and the Tennessee Two. The vocals include Cash at his starkest and most haunting, alternately venting sorrow, scorn, disgust, and anger. On some songs he sings alone, forlorn as the ghostly tribes he recalls. On others he is backed by the eerily beautiful and harmonized hummings, sighs, and moans of the Carter family women.

The album's most famous song is "The Ballad of Ira Hayes," which retells the story of an Indian marine who helped raise the flag at Iwo Jima, but back home in "the land he'd fought to save" dies alcoholic and neglected, facedown in a ditch.[35] Cash's outrage simmers when he delivers lyrics about the "white man's greed" that stole water rights from the Pima Indians. But the outrage positively blazes and singes when he notes that the heroic former solider was allowed on his parched reservation to "raise the flag and lower it, like you'd throw a dog a bone." Hayes was among those immortalized in Joe Rosenthal's photograph of the Stars and Stripes being pushed tall by six soldiers after the bloody battle on the Japanese island. Cash's line about the homeland flag raising, dripping with disgust, suggests that Rosenthal's iconic image was made a travesty by Anglo treatment of the American Indian back in the postwar United States. On "As Long as the Grass Shall Grow," Cash bitterly recalls a treaty with the Senecas signed by George Washington, later broken when the country promised to the Indians till the sun burns out is flooded to make a lake. The lake drowns Indian graveyards and changes "the mint green earth to mud flats, as honor hobbles down." When he proffers the Indian name for this lake, Cash spits each of its three syllables: "Perfidy."

Another piece, "Custer," turns to acidic humor. The golden-maned general may be remembered as a tragic hero from one perspective, but from the perspective of Cash's Native American narrator, he was a "zero" rather than a hero. With military triumphs "he was swimmin'; he killed children, dogs, and women." From this vantage point Custer's defeat at Little Big Horn was "an Indian victory," though dominant history may render it as a "bloody massacree." In the song's last refrain, Cash snorts and chuckles that however distorted Custer's lionized memory may be, "now the general's silent—he got barbered violent."

Other songs on the album reveal not so much rage as a bottomless grief. "Apache Tears" recounts the legendary genesis of the volcanic black pebbles found in Arizona. These are said to be the "petrified, but justified" tears of Apache women and children whose warrior mates and fathers were slaughtered in an ambush by the U.S. army. The album's closing number, "The Vanishing Race," begins with Cash chanting over wearily pounded drums. He so thoroughly inhabits the Indian persona that it sounds as if he is in the thrall of a vision quest, that he has drifted in an out-of-body experience beyond the time and space of a 1960s recording studio. He is himself witnessing the first wagon train crossing the prairie long ago, an eagle floating in emptiness, and the crushing premonition that his race is doomed. The chant returns, bearing all the sorrows of a lost world, drums burbling under it like a choked and dying creek, then fades. The searing album ends, but cannot be forgotten.

Bitter Tears is a feat of empathetic imagination, a masterpiece of storytelling and stark musical artistry. It is Cash at his most brilliant and in crucial ways his most Christian. In the biblical and Augustinian tradition, it is not denial and false innocence that gives new life. It is confession, painful as it may be, that renders personal and collective history truthfully and yet bearably, by the only means that can prevent continued or future harm. Here is how theologian Reinhold Niebuhr, at his epigrammatic best, summarizes the matter:

> Nothing that is worth doing can be achieved in our lifetime; therefore we must be saved by hope. Nothing which is true or beautiful or good makes complete sense in the immediate context of history, therefore we must be saved by faith. Nothing we do, however virtuous, can be accomplished alone; therefore we must be saved by love. No virtuous act is quite as virtuous from the standpoint of our friend or foe as it is from our standpoint. Therefore we must be saved by the final form of love which is forgiveness.[36]

Chapter 6

Violence and Peace

*W*hen *Daniel Boone* premiered on television in 1964, I was seven years old. I recall the episode very dimly. But what is quite clear is that I was disappointed by its ending.

I loved Daniel's coonskin cap and the rousing theme song, punctuated by two gunshots and promising that Boone "was the rippinest, roarinest, fightinest man the frontier ever knew." In the first episode, Boone has established a fort in the Kentucky wilderness. Indians threaten. I expected there to be a climactic battle, the day secured for the settlers by Boone's violent prowess. Instead, our hero went outside the fort's gate (unarmed, if I remember correctly) and calmly negotiated a truce. Peace was established, at least temporarily. Daniel Boone made friends with the Indians, and then the episode was over.

What? No gunfire? No tomahawks thrown? Not so much as a knife fight? I know I grew up only seventy miles from legendary Dodge City and had worn toy six-guns around my diapers, but I'll wager I wasn't the only American boy disappointed that night. Violence—heroic violence—is a staple in American entertainment and in typical conceptions of the nation's history. Daniel Boone settling without a fight seemed unheroic, a bit of a cheat, maybe even vaguely un-American.

I have since learned that the premiere episode depicted someone closer to the real-life Daniel Boone than the Boone of my young imagination. As one biographer flatly puts it, the real-life Daniel Boone "hated killing."[1] He was born to a family of Pennsylvania Quakers. Even though it was already theirs by English law, the Quakers of Pennsylvania had negotiated with and paid native American

99

Indians for title to their land. They also promised the natives all rights and privileges due to other, newer, English-speaking inhabitants of the territory. So Daniel Boone grew up with Indian neighbors and friends. Boone the great woodsman learned the ways of the forest and its creatures from the original American forest dwellers. He never became an Indian hater. Unlike his peers, he refused to take scalps. Near the end of his life he said he had killed no more than three Indians in the whole of his many explorations and adventures. One of his contemporaries declared, "Boone had very little of the war spirit. He never liked to take life and always avoided it when he could."[2]

There can be no doubt of violence in American history. But Daniel Boone's transmogrification, in cultural memory, to the "rippinest, roarinest, fightinest" man on the frontier is a case study in how American violence has been exaggerated and idealized. Boone died in 1820, nine years before the first of Andrew Jackson's two terms as president.[3] Jackson would institute Indian Removal, ratifying nearly seventy treaties resulting in the forced movement of 45,000 Native Americans from their land. Jacksonian Democrats popularized the term "Manifest Destiny" to render the westward expansion of Anglo Americanism, with all its attendant violence, not simply justifiable but natural and inevitable. The real estate developer John Filson, who wanted to sell property in Kentucky, published the first account of Boone's pioneering in 1784, thereby (and incidentally) creating "the first nationally viable statement of a myth of the frontier."[4] Filson's chronicle made Boone more reckless and readily violent than he actually was, and later Jacksonian-era narratives ratcheted up the violence several notches. Davy Crockett, the Tennessean who would die in the Alamo in 1836, modeled his public persona after minstrel show depictions of Daniel Boone, politicking in buckskins (like those worn by Boone and his minstrel show impersonators) and a coonskin cap (Boone actually wore a beaver hat; Crockett wore the coonskin only in his public persona).[5] Crockett was a man more of the Jacksonian and post-Jacksonian eras. While Boone hunted for subsistence, Crockett reveled in killing. There is a tenebrous wastefulness in Crockett's depiction of his own hunting. Crockett cared for the head count and could leave carcasses to rot. In his autobiography he boasted of taking 105 bears in a single season, on one occasion dispatching three in "less than half an hour." He bragged that he one day shot six deer and left them moldering in his wake as he pursued other game.[6] Crockett evidences joy in violence for the sake of violence, destruction to no end but destruction. He foreshadows westbound train passengers passing through herds of buffalo up to 120 miles long, leaning out their carriage windows and gunning down as many beasts as they could. Even more disturbingly, Crockett's is the mentality of the gunfighter who adds a notch to his pistol handle for every man he kills.

Lethal violence, of course, is all too common to human history, and not unique to America. The uniqueness of the American attitude toward violence can be understood only when our violence is juxtaposed with the dangerous assurance of our innocence, our confidence that we (or at least the "good guys" among us) will always employ violence justifiably and proportionately. What is also unique to Americans is the idealization and ongoing mythic appropriation of our frontier heritage, and so the degree to which violent resolution continues to attract us as especially heroic, necessary, and efficacious. It is these conditions that can begin to explain how an American officer in Vietnam could remark—without any intention of irony—that "we had to destroy the village in order to save it." These conditions begin to make sense of the widespread American expectation that, in the Iraq of 2003, we could unleash the "shock and awe" of our unprecedented military might, occupy cities by force, and still be greeted with flowers, as utterly benevolent liberators.

Inside American adults are little boys and girls clad in coonskin caps, mesmerized by the allure of idealized violence. We might just as well admit it: no small part of the phenomenon of Johnny Cash was and is his aura of violence. The Man in Black could be going to church or mourning people in bondage. But in the same dark, long-tailed coat, he could also be a frontier undertaker, a figure redolent of death. With that sneer, that facial scar (actually the result of botched dental surgery), that smoldering anger, here was a masculine presence not to be ignored or taken lightly. No wonder people assumed, mistakenly, that he really had been in prison. He had sung the song before, but the live jailhouse rendition of "Folsom Prison Blues" was a hit all over again, and epitomized Cash's 1968 comeback. We could believe it when Cash's narrator declared he "shot a man in Reno, just to watch him die."[7]

When producer Rick Rubin shepherded Cash's second, 1994 comeback, he focused on Cash's image as an "outlaw figure," understanding outlawry as the "essence of rock 'n' roll."[8] The rock music media responded obligingly, running menacing photos that emphasized Cash's dangerous side. The representation of Cash as a violent (or at least potentially violent) man was not conjured out of thin air. Before he became known as the Man in Black, the young Cash pioneered what would become the rock and roll tradition of trashing hotels where he and his band lodged. On various occasions (and at different hotels—it got so that they were hardly allowed in the same one twice), Cash and his cohort flushed exploding cherry bombs down toilets, sawed a room's furniture and stacked it like firewood, filled a bathtub with Jell-O, borrowed the fire ax to hew a doorway in a room's wall, smashed antique chandeliers, spread hay and horse manure (at the Waldorf Astoria, no less), stuck a bowie knife in a print of the *Mona Lisa*, and fired a "signal cannon" down a hallway. Cash did not confine his violence to hotels. He once used his microphone stand to shatter sixty footlights at the Grand Ole Opry. In hazes of amphetamines and rage, he crashed a series of cars, sank a boat, overturned a tractor, and (accidentally) started a forest fire in Los Padres National Forest. There is no record of him ever assaulting a person (his Air Force buddies remembered him as tamer than most soldiers out on the town), and some of his antics were more prankish than destructive. But a dark yearning to wreck and destroy ran through much of his activity. Country singer Waylon Jennings recalls himself and Cash in Buffalo, climbing into a Cadillac driven by a man who promised to find them drugs and women. Jennings thought matters were progressing as hoped, but the impatient Cash sarcastically complimented the driver on his pretty car. While he spoke, Cash repeatedly slit the leather seats with his pocketknife. As Waylon said, "A lot of that shit was mean."[9]

Cash recognized his meanness and fought to contain it. He insisted (quite sensibly) on maintaining a line between art and life.

It was one thing to play on the aura of violence, another to act out violently. He knew, for instance, that when he sang the line about shooting a man to watch him die at Folsom, the burst of applause heard on record at the delivery of that line was added later, in the studio, by the record company. The prison audience itself did not offer raucous, audible approval.[10] More significantly, Cash's songs depicting violence rarely idealized or glorified it. His doers of violence suffer remorse, torment, and imprisonment or execution as consequences of their actions ("Folsom Prison Blues," "Delia's Gone," "Cocaine Blues"). They can die foolishly, trying to prove their manhood ("Don't Take Your Guns to Town"). In the chilling "I Hung My Head," the narrator toys with his brother's rifle and takes aim (for "practice") at a distant man on horseback. Before he knew it, the rifle "went off in my hands," as if it has a sinister will all its own. Later, in the courtroom, he confesses to himself as well as the jury that he killed senselessly, simply for the feeling of "the power of death over life." Here violence is naked and repulsive. It has no efficacy except to orphan the victim's children and widow his wife, "all for no reason."[11]

This is not to say that Cash imagined all violence was without efficacy. He was proud of his own military service and often commemorated American military battles in song. Yet even in the realm of heroic warfare, Cash can evidence ambivalence. His 1972 track "The Big Battle" receives little comment but is a remarkable piece of folkloric but deromanticizing songwriting. It is the closest thing Cash ever wrote to an outright antiwar song. In it, a young Civil War soldier hears the shooting fade out and is ready to disarm, thinking the conflict is done. His commanding officer is more seasoned and rebukes the younger soldier. The physical warfare may be done, but the "big battle" is yet to come and will span over decades. It will, says the officer, "rage in the bosom of mother and sweetheart and wife / Brother and sister and daughter will grieve for the rest of their lives." The soldier is a quick study and agrees that this arduous struggle of sorrow and memory "has only begun"—the rest of it will "cover the part that has blackened the sun." Dropping gun and saber, he reports himself ready for the real battle of life after the profound destruction of warfare.[12]

⸙⸙⸙⸙⸙⸙⸙

Cash, then, testifies to another contradictory hallmark of the American character. We find violence compelling in many ways, and often render our history as hinging on the noble employment of violence. Yet we are never entirely at home with violence; we cannot always idealize it and sometimes we (and our poets) cannot resist tearing away the gauzy veil of romance surrounding it. Why do Cash and so many other Americans suffer this contradiction? There is of course no simple account, but surely a significant shadow looming over our uneasiness and ambivalence about violence is that of Jesus Christ.

I will not pretend that the church and Christianity—including the American church and Christianity—have been by any stretch predominantly pacifist. Yet it is very difficult for any thoughtful Christian to get around the biblical depiction of Jesus and his work on the cross as fundamentally nonviolent. In historical terms, Jesus the Nazarene lived in a world where violent rebellion against the occupying Romans was a very real option. The Palestinian Jews had attempted it before; Jesus' circle of disciples included those who thought these people should again take up the sword; and only a few decades after his death the Jews of Roman-occupied Israel would again rebel violently. Jesus chose not to employ violence in his mission and, exactly through his determination to be the object rather than the subject of violent death, was exalted as Lord, "to the glory of God the Father" (Phil. 2:6–11). Far from obscuring Jesus' participation in the true power of God, his "lifting up" on the cross is the very act meant to "draw all people" to him as the Messiah and Son of Man (John 12:32–33; also 3:14). Of course, for his past and current followers, Jesus' death on the cross was unique in its cosmic significance. His death and resurrection alone reconcile God and humanity, and definitively expose and overcome the world's brokenness and evil. Yet it is exactly here, in assumption of the cross, that his followers are called to be like him. As the theologian John Howard Yoder puts it,

> [T]here is no *general* concept of living like Jesus in the New Testament. According to universal tradition, Jesus was not married;

yet when the apostle Paul, advocate *par excellence* of the life 'in Christ,' argues at length for celibacy or for a widow's not remarrying (1 Cor 7), it never occurs to him to appeal to Jesus' example, even as one of many arguments. Jesus is thought in his earlier life to have worked as a carpenter; yet never, even when he explains at length why he earns his own way as an artisan (1 Cor 9), does it come to Paul's mind that he is imitating Jesus. Jesus' association with villagers, his drawing his illustrations from the life of the peasants and the fishermen, his leading disciples to desert places and mountaintops, have often been appealed to as examples by the advocates of rural life and church camping; but not in the New Testament. . . .

There is thus but one realm in which the concept of imitation holds—but there it holds in every strand of the New Testament literature and all the more strikingly by virtue of the absence of parallels in other realms. This is at the point of the concrete social meaning of the cross in its relation to enmity and power. Servanthood replaces dominion, forgiveness absorbs hostility. Thus—and only thus—are we bound by New Testament thought to "be like Jesus."[13]

The power of God anticipated in Israel and revealed on the cross is the paradoxical power of vulnerability. It admits that we are but creatures and not controllers of our destiny, that we are dependent on God and one another for our survival and prospering. It sees the course of history determined not by lethal violence but by nonviolent suffering and compassion. Accordingly, it is difficult to read the story of Jesus, and its call to take up our cross and follow him, and not expect that Christians should live (and die) with a presumption against violence—even if not its absolute abandonment as a reluctant, infrequent, and last resort. In the words of the nonpacifist theologian William Placher, "In a broken and complex world, we Christians may sometimes find ourselves driven to force and even violence in spite of our best intentions, but we need to acknowledge that to choose such alternatives is always to admit a failure of imagination, a concession to weakness, always to have betrayed the image of the power of love we have encountered in the powerless Jesus on the cross." Or, as Pope Benedict XVI recently expressed it, "It is thus understood that nonviolence, for Christians, is not mere tactical behavior but a person's way of being, the attitude of one who is convinced of God's love and power, who is not afraid to confront evil with the weapons of love and truth alone. . . . Herein lies the novelty of the Gospel, which changes the world without making noise."[14]

For the first three centuries of its life, before it was sanctioned by Roman imperial power, the Christian church embodied a presumption for peace and against violence. Across much of their subsequent history, Christians have undeniably and frequently availed themselves of coercion and violence. Yet the biblical witness of Christ and his cross always sat uneasily with the employment of violence. And in the last three centuries Christendom has wilted, so that all churches have officially relinquished their own coercive power and endorsed the freedom of religion. In these circumstances, even (or especially?) popes can speak of nonviolence as the Christian's basic "way of being." If this is so, what occurs when the Christian who also happens to be an American revisits our nation's deep attraction to violence? Put directly, what might the church now have to say in response to the American myths of violence as redemptive and regenerative, a force that cleanses and brings new life?

ᔕᔕᔕᔕᔕᔕᔕ

With a cross-shadowed presumption against violence, the church in America might well take a second look at its nation's (and its own) estimate of the true potentials of lethal force, and particularly warfare. "Realism" is typically thought to be on the side of recourse—more or less regular—to violence, but it is arguable that America has been insufficiently realistic about violence, consistently overrating its necessity and efficacy.

In terms of necessity, we have understood our frontier history as one marked by constant violence. Our literature and other media depict the frontier as a site of necessary and copious brutality. Yet, as we have already glimpsed in relation to Daniel Boone, the American "wilderness" and its "settlement" were not always characterized by lethal enmity between Native Americans and Anglo American immigrants. Frequently there was cooperation and, as in the case of the original Pilgrims, Indian aid and guidance were essential to Anglo survival. Furthermore, the comparatively nonviolent settlements of the Australian and Canadian frontiers show that the extent of blood-letting done on America's frontier was not necessary, not simply the "only way" settlement could have been accomplished. And even as the violence on American frontiers did exceed that in other national histories, we have exaggerated it. Frontier towns settled rather quickly, usually up and running with schools, churches, and law and order within a decade or two of their foundings. And the amount of blood spilled while these towns were at the (brief) wildest is much greater in popular imagination than in historical reality. One study of five leading Kansas cattle towns at the peak of their rowdiness (1870–1885) found 45 homicides during that span, an average of three per year, or one and a half every cattle driving season. The high-est annual number was five murders (at Dodge City in 1878, at Ellsworth in 1873). Or consider other famous Old West sites of law-lessness and abandon: Deadwood, South Dakota, registered its most violent year in 1876, with four deaths; Tombstone, Arizona, peaked at five deaths in 1881.[15]

This is mortality enough, for sure, and I am not trying to reenvision the American frontier as a pacifist's holiday. Actual history, however, is an indication that frontier violence—even in the wildest towns at their wildest times—did not occur regularly on a daily, weekly, or even monthly basis. The killing of fellow men and women looms much larger in our national imagination and memory than it did in the gen-uine day-to-day lives of our ancestors. Settlement not only could but often did occur without recourse to severe levels of violence. In the Oklahoma Land Run of 1889, for instance, 15,000 would-be land claimants—almost everyone armed—completed the run with no killings, no gunshot wounds, not even a fistfight. Six months passed before the territory recorded its first homicide. The much more typi-cal and prevalent occurrence for Anglo settlers was not violence but unrelieved loneliness and boredom. There were no newspapers, let alone electronic media. A family Bible was the extent of many homes' libraries. Neighbors or a store or town were usually so distant they were visited only occasionally. Besides work on the farm (and the plowboy, not the cowboy, is far and away statistically the dominant figure in America's settlement), there was very little to do.[16] In sum, the actual violence levied in the nation's Anglo settlement was in large part not strictly necessary, and in all events we vastly overestimate the regularity and amount of violence, "necessary" or otherwise, that actually unfolded.

But what about our wars, from the War of Independence on? Here debates about "necessity" rapidly turn extremely speculative, because such a multitude of historical factors is in play. It is at least arguable that American's independence from Britain might have been achieved without a war; nineteenth-century Canada achieved its independence gradually and peaceably. In our own time, the majority and black citizens of South Africa assumed government without an all-out war. There is clearly no universal, ironclad natural or historical law that war is necessary for the founding of an independent nation. But particular, actual history bristles with contingencies. Perhaps if the U.S. had not fought and defeated the British in the eighteenth century, proving they could be militarily repulsed by a colony, the Canadians would have had to fight in the nineteenth century. And of course there are arguments that the British nation was on the whole a more humane culture than other occupiers and invaders in history. As this objection is often put, would Gandhi's methods of nonviolent resistance have worked against the Nazis? Thus we fall immediately into hypothetical castings and recastings of the scores of factors, great and small, that combine to lead into full-blown shooting wars. In such complex, contingent, specific historical circumstances, there are many arguments about the necessity or nonnecessity of a particular war, but few if any clear conclusions. So here I believe the more compelling and constructive conversation to be had concerns the actual efficacy of violence, and more especially warfare.

My suggestion is that we Americans, in thrall to the myths of redemptive and regenerative violence, tend to be notably unrealistic in facing and assessing the costs of war, costs moral and spiritual as well as economic and political. We idealize violence and look away from the ugliness of actual battlefields as thoroughly as we can. We discourage literature, photographs, or other media showing our dead or mutilated soldiers and the "collateral damage" of killed or maimed noncombatants, including children. At the same time, we overestimate the resolution and closure war brings to difficult situations of conflict. With a bias toward believing violence to be outstandingly effective, we fail to look at our wars not only closely but in terms of the longer view. Thus we speak of the Civil War as "settling" the issue of slavery, as if slavery had and has no ongoing effects, as if the brutalizing and hateful mind-sets birthed and steeped in American slavery did not continue to manifest themselves after 1865. We tell ourselves war decisively and effectively brings peace, and ignore the reality that war often begets more war. The Spanish-American War (1898) led directly into the much bloodier Philippine-American War (1899–1902). World War I (1914–18) was, from the American vantage point, the war fought to end all war, but ended with no neat closure or profound resolution; its "closure" in fact set the stage for the even more destructive catastrophe of World War II, just over two decades later (1939–45). Our American idealization of violence extends to retrospection, to distortion as we look back on past wars. For instance, Americans often recall World War II as a war we undertook partly to save European Jews from the Holocaust. That U.S. involvement was key to liberating the Jews (an admirable effect, indeed), I do not doubt or decry. But our nation's *intentions* upon entering the war were not gilded by this noble aim. Government, media, and churches were aware before 1941 of the plight of European Jews and took little or no interest. Frank Capra's exhortatory and massively exposed "Why We Fight" films made no mention of Hitler's attacks on Jews. In the three international conferences where the Allies strategized their war aims, no leader spoke out about the plight of the Jews.[17] In this and similar instances, the lies and self-deception bred in and by war continue well after the shooting has ended.

Christians beholden to a presumption for peace will insist on truthfulness when anticipating or evaluating war. The American penchant for idealizing violence obscures the spiritual and moral costs of war, exaggerates its powers of resolution, and clouds the honest memory of it. Such conditions not only dismiss the Christian tradition's very real (if minority) witness of pacifism; they disable the dominant Christian tradition of just war. This they do by preventing assessment of circumstances that determine whether or not a given war can be (or was) conducted justly, according to the Christian church's longstanding criteria for a just war.

For Christians and other citizens, the idealization of violence today has pressing political ramifications and effects. There is no guarantee democracy and empire, especially militarized empire, are compatible. The Founding Fathers saw war as a serious threat to the openness and national self-control that democracy demands. They worried about militarization, to the degree that George Washington disbanded the army after assuming the presidency. Much later, in the 1950s, President Dwight Eisenhower, himself a soldier, warned strenuously against further development of a "military-industrial complex." Today's American War on Terror, with its utterly unrealistic aims such as ridding the world of evil and its pronounced inclination to govern by fear—internally as well as externally—exacerbates the worst tendencies of idealized violence and cripples democracy. Though I think American democracy is already gravely imperiled, not all my fellow citizens (and Christian believers) agree. What appears patently foolish is any degree of complacency about the successful and felicitous union of militaristic empire and democracy.[18]

※※※※※※

There is another angle from which to approach the role of violence (and peace) in the American identity and character. It is manifestly the case that violence has played a real role in our American history. In response, I have argued that violence has not been as prevalent or as efficacious as often thought. But now, for the sake of discussion, let us grant that the myths of redemptive and regenerative violence have had authentic utility in the history of the United States. Perhaps these myths (that violence can redeem, can bring new life) steeled our ancestors, helping them to launch out into the unknown and (for them) chaotic wilderness. Perhaps the myths gave them courage to go on, even in the face of the very real possibility of death to themselves. Perhaps these myths, in the sense that myths can be, *were true*. Then perhaps, symbolically and comprehensively, they depicted the world as it really was in a comparatively raw, undeveloped, intensely conflictual time and place. Suppose all that, and still we are beholden to ask: do the myths of violence have utility in the present and future of the United States and the world? On a globe where there is no "new world" to be discovered, or developed, or exploited, is the courage that we need the courage to dominate, to conquer, to coercively gain and maintain control? In a world that we now see to have ecological limits, and which humanity has the technological capacity to burn to a bare cinder in a matter of hours—in this world, are the myths true? Can violence ultimately redeem and bring new life?

To prevent these important questions from remaining merely abstract, I want to focus on two particular instances or aspects of American violence. First, we will ask if the concept and practice of honor—of communal esteem and good reputation—is still well served (whether or not it really ever was) by a tight association with prickly masculinity and the willingness to kill or maim in response to insult. Second, we will bear down on the viability and truthfulness of the myth of regenerative violence in a world not of boundless "resources" but of undeniable limits; we will do this with the aid of an early scrutinization of the American embrace of this myth, Herman Melville's 1851 novel *Moby-Dick*.

As regards honor, one of the main sources of its ethos in the Old South was the medieval tradition of chivalry. This knightly code extolled charity to the poor and protection of the weak; it also expected fearlessness in physical combat and a veritable ferocity to see the right done. In the American South, gentlemen liked to think of themselves as knightly. Worthy (male) youth were called "knights," and jousting tournaments were popular, especially in Virginia and South Carolina. Whatever its pacific and amorous elements, "Historically, chivalry—medieval, southern, or other—has rested on violence. . . . Medieval chivalry . . . has a bloody-minded side manifested in a 'prickly sense of honor,' an 'insistence on autonomy,' and a 'quick recourse to violence.' "[19] The ready resort to violence made southern honor volatile enough, but to really reckon with its explosive potential, we need to note as well how utterly valuable and, in a sense, fragile, honor was considered to be. Honor was the individual's, the family's, and the community's most prized attribute. It was inestimably precious, "to be protected against stain at every cost."[20]

It was also understood as a kind of inviolable absolute; to lose face or have honor questioned—on any single occasion, no matter how trivial, or in any part, no matter how small—was to risk loss of its possession altogether and irretrievably. Thus honor was like an antiquated Grecian urn, something simply beyond price and at the same time easily breakable: to let it drop once, and only once, could be catastrophic.

Here, of course, lie the origins and rationale for the code duello. You might assault my mother or merely accuse me of cheating at cards. Either way, my honor—my manhood—hangs in doubt until I call you out for a faceoff with pistols. On this account of honor, a man might be pompous, boorish, and considerably provocative, yet retain his dignity and honor so long as he was ready to issue (or accept) the challenge to a duel. So it was that in the Bible-venerating South, a guidebook for duelists could explicitly deplore "the Christian doctrine of turning the other cheek," regarding such behavior as "utterly repugnant to those feelings which nature and education have implanted in human nature." For the same guidebook, outlawing the duel would endanger an entire way of life. Since "words are not satisfaction for words," only physical violence was adequate recourse for disagreements.[21]

Even as dueling was eventually made illegal, what remained was the mindset of honor as ultimately proved by reckless physical "courage" and aggressiveness. The code duello was replaced by a degenerate version of itself, one which trashed the code and kept the duello. The comparatively civilized ethic of the duel devolved into more random gunplay and knifing, as well as the unrestrainable custom of "shooting-on-sight" someone thought to have aggrieved one's honor. Historian C. Vann Woodward argues that, "if anything," violence was more characteristic of the post-Reconstruction New South than of the Old South. In 1890, there were 16 recorded homicides in highly populated Massachusetts, but 65 in Virginia, 69 in North Carolina, 88 in Kentucky, 92 in Georgia, and 115 in Tennessee. Italy had the highest homicide rate in Europe; America's south central states, with a total population one-third the size of Italy's, had more prisoners incarcerated with murder charges. Says Woodward: "The South seems to have been one of the most violent communities of comparable size in all Christendom."[22] Migrating southerners carried the attitudes of degenerated chivalry and the code duello to Texas. From there they moved northwest with the great cattle drives of the later nineteenth century. The code of the West demanded the avenging of all insults, real or imagined, with violence.[23]

Such are the taproots of the ongoing American tendency to equate honor with masculinity, masculinity with physical courage and dominance, and courage with the ready resort to violence. In such a schema, honor (reputation, communal esteem) for the female can only be derivative. A woman accesses and shares in the highest level of honor by associating herself with a physically powerful man. So long as violent action is considered the final and ultimate guarantor of honor and its security ("words are not satisfaction for words"), and so long as the average male has superior upper-body strength to that of the average female, honor in its supreme exemplification will be masculine. Such patriarchalism made some kind of sense in an earlier world that thought the female to be, literally and biologically, a defective male. In a world that knows different and that sees women lead effectively every day, in all manner of roles, masculinized honor seems (because it is) arbitrary. In the final analysis the cowboy code can be pronounced nothing other than nihilistic (might makes right, period) or juvenile (when Daniel Boone does not fire powder, it's one thing for a seven-year-old to suffer disappointment, another if a grown-up does the same). So much for the truthfulness of the myth of redemptive violence in our day and age.

In terms of its utility, we need look only so far as the hyperviolence of many of our inner cities, our urban war zones. There are the most direct and full-blown current descendants of the code duello to be found on American soil.[24] Inner-city gangs are our contemporary equivalent of Old West outlaw bands and posses. Range wars are replaced by turf wars. Gangbangers explicitly see themselves as "players" in a brutal and sometimes lethal "game," accruing some kind of honor via their willingness to brave bullets and to kill. Police stations are designated "forts" on the wild urban frontiers. The initials D.C. (as in District of Columbia) are taken for "Dodge City." This city is the capital of our country. We are now in the twenty-first century. There just might be a better way, more constructive myths to live by.

༄༄༄༄༄༄

Now we turn to the myth of regenerative violence in the same spirit. For the sake of discussion, I will grant that this myth seemed to make some real sense for an earlier America. To Anglo Americans, the vast continent before them seemed almost empty of inhabitants. It stretched westward, on and on. Remember that it was not until 1804, when Thomas Jefferson sent Lewis and Clark on their expedition, that European Americans began to get a real picture of just how far westward the continent stretched, of its magnificently varied topography, and even of its curious menagerie of animals. Immigrants had time after time commented on how abundant game animals and wild fruit were in this seemingly endless expanse of forest and plain. What would later be called its natural resources appeared inexhaustible. Who could imagine running out of fresh water in a huge land of so many rivers and lakes and wells that never went dry? If a given homestead somehow did exhaust its bounty, or merely if prospects might be better elsewhere, there was—until early decades of the twentieth century—always "undeveloped," "virgin," open land elsewhere. So much of the vast land and its treasures was new, just waiting for its wealth to be tapped. The new treasures kept being discovered or accessed, again and again: the Louisiana Purchase (1803) opens up hundreds of millions of acres of rich farmland across the great Mississippi River basin; mountains of gold are uncovered in 1829 (in the Appalachians) and in the 1840s (California); the petroleum industry launches in 1859 and continues to find fresh reservoirs through the 1950s. The most extraordinary thing about Americans, the astute French observer Alexis de Tocqueville said after visiting in the 1830s, "is the soil that supports them." This "boundless continent," untouched "as in the first days of the creation," appeared limitless in what it could give (or have wrenched) from the bottomless vaults of its bounty. And, "All that was offered to view in those enchanted places seemed prepared for the needs of men or calculated for his pleasures."[25]

So the "enchanted" land is vast and seemingly inexhaustibly rich. But (again speaking from the European American viewpoint) it needs for its proper development hard work. Nature may be abundantly attractive, but she is not easy. She gives up her trees no more readily than we lose our rooted teeth to a dentist. And thousands, millions of trees, must be cut down and extracted. Nature's gold, her silver, her cotton, her oil— none of this is harvested without backbreaking labor. Furthermore, this land needs men and women willing to gamble, to leave all that is familiar in hopes of having and being more in an unknown elsewhere. They risk not only fortune (such as it may be), but hunger, undoctored sickness, and death at the whim of human and beast. They go to a place of great, undreamt promise, but promise that cannot be realized without the bravery and determination and ruthlessness of conquerors.

All this is the atmosphere, the air gasped into the lungs of the myth of regenerative violence. The land holds abundant life, yet it is life that can be realized only by persistent and overpowering force. Violence gives life to a place that is otherwise dormant, asleep as if in death. Violence regenerates. Rapacious exploitation is necessary, exciting, and praiseworthy.

ᏗᏗᏗᏗᏗᏗᏗ

Herman Melville published *Moby-Dick* in 1851. It is a, if not *the*, great American novel. Generations of Americans read and reread it because it helps us see what it is to be an American. As a book, it is itself a whale, gigantic in themes and possibilities of interpretation. Its aspect germane to our consideration is Melville's revelatory scrutiny of the national myth of regenerative violence.

At the center of the story is of course a "colossal hunt" for the great sperm whale Moby-Dick. The whale is a protean image. It literally embodies substantial riches, with its huge reservoir of oil. Less literally, it is both hunted and hunter, sacrificial victim and wrathful god. It is a "beast like an island or continent in the middle of the ocean"— the great American territory itself.[26] Like America, Moby-Dick can yield vast returns, but these returns can be realized only through violence. Like America, Moby-Dick is dangerous and wild. To pursue Moby/America entails venturing onto the infinite ocean, which Melville repeatedly describes as a sprawling prairie frontier. The Nantucket whaling man "lives on the sea, as prairie cocks in the prairie." Icy seas appear as "an unbounded prairie sheeted with driven snow," and serene seas are reminiscent of waves of rustling prairie grass. A terrible storm roars around a lost whaling boat "like a white fire upon the prairie." The whaling man hunts for oil, "even as the traveller on the prairie hunts for his own supper of game." Roaming these endless marine frontiers, Moby-Dick is a "moss-bearded Daniel Boone." Humpback whales have humps like the buffalo's, and at one point of the all-consuming quest, the ship's crew's "wild eyes" meet Captain Ahab's, "as the bloodshot eyes of prairie wolves meet the eyes of their leader while they are hunting bison."[27]

So in a sense Melville is retelling the story of America and the conquest of its frontiers. The whalers go forth into the unknown, led by a man of irresistible passion who will risk all for the hunt. Violence appears to be regenerative—it yields food for the physical body, but more profoundly and spiritually, it animates, providing something to live (and die) for. Yet Melville's story is much more searching. It does not quit with a glance at the surface of the myth of regenerative violence. It delves deeper, and as it does, the novel and the myth itself becomes dark and disturbing. The violence does not appear so life-giving when it turns wasteful, as in the chapter where the crew uses sharp tools to cut and kill "incalculable hosts" of sharks near the ship. More significantly, Melville pushes us to examine the myth of redemptive violence on a wider screen, over the longer term. Violence may immediately seem to animate and bring life, but its destruction is ultimately self-destructive. The energy and life it feeds on is our own energy and life. The ship *Pequod,* garnished with the teeth of sperm whales on her open bulwarks, is herself a "cannibal of a craft," "tricking herself forth in the chased bones of her enemies." And the whale hunters themselves gradually go savage, reducing their allegiances to "the King of the Cannibals." (Early on, Ishmael decides, "Better sleep with a sober cannibal than a drunken Christian.")[28]

In the end, Ahab catches up with the object of his quest. The whalers harpoon Moby-Dick. But the captain is entangled in the harpoon's line and dragged to his death by the whale. Indeed, the entire ship and crew (excepting Ishmael, who alone lives to tell the tale) goes down. The conquest results finally in the destruction of the would-be conquerors, who, in retrospect, were caught up in an incoherent passion, plying the ocean's "infinite blueness to seek out the

thing that might destroy them." Dedicated to this illusory and cata-
clysmic mission, the *Pequod* is as doomed as her namesake, a "celebrated tribe of Massachusetts Indians, now extinct as the ancient
Medes." The vanquished American Indians do enjoy a kind of grim
revenge. With the ship sliding beneath the water, the Indian Tashtego
desperately hammers a flag onto the sinking mast. As only "a red arm
and hammer" hover above the sea's surface, a "sky-hawk" dives to
peck at the flag and the "submerged savage" feels and clamps its wing
to the mast. If we take this bird, with its "archangelic shrieks" and its
"imperial beak," as an eagle, then the very symbol of American freedom and life goes down with the ship.[29] In Melville's gloomy brood-
ing, so ends the American story. The myth of regenerative violence,
played out to its ending, is exposed as all-consuming and degenera-
tive. Its destruction is so total, its decimation so absolute, that all that
truly is and brings life collapses beneath the primeval chaos, descend-
ing and disintegrating under the funereal "great shroud of the sea
[that] rolled on as it rolled five thousand years ago."[30]

Thus the *Pequod*ian quest of regenerative violence is a kind of anti-
creation story, as in Melville's time theologians assumed that the
earth was created five thousand years before, when the God of Genesis called it forth from the "formless void" and out of dark waters.
More, the violence of *Moby-Dick* is a reversal of the life-giving—the
truly regenerative—death and resurrection of Jesus Christ. The climactic chase of the whale lasts three days, the same period of time
Jesus was entombed. On the third day in the Gospels comes new life;
on the third day in the novel comes consummatory annihilation. In
Christian profession, Christ rises never to die again. In *Moby-Dick*'s
disintegrating universe of regenerative violence, Ahab prophesies
that the whale will surface again after two days' submersion: "Aye,
men, he'll rise once more,—but only to spout his last!"[31]

* * * * * * *

Of course, the actual American story did not end in Melville's age,
and it has not ended yet. But I take Melville's tale as cautionary and
admonitory. At some level, his prophetic vision pierced to the heart

of one of our country's most prized myths and saw it to be ultimately incoherent and corrupt. He truly was prescient, writing in a day when it took real imagination to envision a time when America's natural treasures might be exhausted, when the ghosts of the former occupants of this continent might see their vanquishers vanquished. Today it does not require so much imagination. The toxic wages of pollution, the threats of global warming, the sucking sound of the last remnants of oil swirling down the drain—these realities surround us. We know and at the most can try only to deny that there are limits to the American soil, American aquifers, and the other gifts of nature. If (and to a degree) America as we know it was built by exploitation, wastefulness, and heedless destruction, then the nation cannot subsist or endure by the same means.

The myth of regenerative violence, however true or helpful it might once have been, is no longer serviceable or constructive. This is the case not only ecologically but in terms of warfare. Realism is no longer on the side of those who dismiss a vision of human existence enduring through peaceableness rather than war. Technologically, human ingenuity has birthed weapons that can destroy the world several times over. Moreover, whatever kind of Strangelovian sense "mutually assured destruction" may have made when two nuclear superpowers squared off against one another, all sense of balance and reasonable control is lost in a world of several nuclear powers.[32] And even lesser, nonnuclear weapons are massively destructive of persons and property, noncombatants and nonstrategic property as well as combatants and strategic property.

Alongside technological developments must be recognized the growth of democracy. Democracy has brought not only the creation of civilian armies (rather than those of the aristocracy and professional soldiers), but a sense of an entire population's participation in and responsibility for war's prosecution. I am referring not simply to the power of the ballot box, but to the rise of guerilla warfare and "people's wars." In an age of widespread democratic ideals (however feebly realized), populaces have discovered they can disrupt and bog down the efforts of occupying enemies by hiding their own combatants, continually provisioning them while the occupiers run out of rations, and passively or actively obstructing and hindering occupiers on a daily basis in myriad small ways. As was seen in China, Vietnam, and (USSR-era) Afghanistan, people's war is the way non-Western people found to defend themselves "against the awesome technical superiority of the superpowers."[33] And as the United States has learned in post-2003 Iraq, all the "smart bombs" or "shock-and-awe" fire-power in the world cannot guarantee a successful occupation.

These technological and democratizing developments have not, of course, rendered warfare obsolete overnight. What they have done is reveal that war too has limits. Militarization and military actions or reactions will not and cannot of themselves "decide" or resolve seri-ous conflicts. You can be the most powerful force in the history of the world militarily, not even remotely approached in this regard by any of your contemporaries, and still be terribly insecure. In fact, you can be even more frightened than you were before such circumstances applied: just look at post-9/11 America.

ᚷᚷᚷᚷᚷᚷᚷ

Such prudential and pragmatic arguments have their place, and I am not ashamed to consider them. I think John Paul II spoke sensibly when he said, "Today, the scale and the horror of modern warfare—whether nuclear or not—makes it totally unacceptable as a means of settling differences between nations. War should belong to the tragic past, to history; it should find no place on humanity's agenda for the future."[34] At the same time, it is crucial I make it clear that for Chris-tians the pragmatic argument is not central. What is central for Chris-tians is the witness of Jesus Christ, and that is the case whatever technological or sociological developments transpire. It is because of Jesus Christ that the Christian has a presumption for peace and against violence—that is true not only now, in democracies and under the threat of nuclear apocalypse; it was the case before, in monarchies and imperial dynasties and feudalisms, when the most destructive weapon at hand was the crossbow. The more the American church takes seriously the example and call of Christ, and the derivative pre-sumption against violence, the more it is likely to find itself in ten-sion with those in government and with fellow U.S. citizens in these insecure times and increasingly militarized climate. Simply to take just-war theory and discipline seriously, let alone Christian pacifism, will make the church sufficiently skeptical of the resort to warfare to raise searching questions about Christian participation in and endorsement of any given war our government may propose (or impose). These questions will in turn ripple out into the surrounding culture, and may urge it along in reconsidering the viability, if not the truth, of the myth of regenerative violence.

Along the way, Christians should not be bashful in helping America to remember that violence is not the nation's only tradition. In no small part, America really has tried to pursue peace. American democracy can itself be seen as a kind of peace movement, a secularization of the ecclesially centered experiments in early New England and Pennsylvania. At his death, George Washington was eulogized as a man of peace, and praised for disbanding the army after the War of Independence. Other founders, like John Adams, were wary of standing armies and the consequences of warfare.[35] American democracy is not a naive attempt to ignore or deny conflict, but a mature willingness to face and engage it, and to do so without resorting to lethal violence. Democracy encourages working out or through or with conflict nonviolently, letting various people have an effective voice. War is not democracy's highest aspiration or crowning moment; war is what happens when democracy fails. Something similar might be said about the free market: just how free is any market propped up by military force?

Surely the influences of Christianity and democracy (and their union) help to account for the fact that the modern practice of organized nonviolent politics and social change originated and grew in the United States. The abolitionist movement was sparked and led by Christians such as William Lloyd Garrison and Sojourner Truth. (Tolstoy, in his own writing on nonviolence, owed much to the abolitionists.) In addition to the Sermon on the Mount, Gandhi was inspired by the Christian abolitionist Americans and others, such as Henry David Thoreau.[36] Then there is the deeply Christian and deeply American thought and action of the great Martin Luther King Jr. Clearly we have not learned all he had to teach us. It will take a long, hard while yet. In the meantime, may our hope and our courage be sustained by King's faith that "the arc of the moral universe is long but it bends toward justice."[37]

Chapter 7

On Baptism, Patriotism, and Being a Christian in Public

I began this book with the promise that Christian, theological convictions and practices could illuminate a series of contradictions at the heart of the American character. I hope my efforts have been successful, however feebly, at suggesting Christian cultural criticism has something to bring to the currently urgent discussion about what America is and where it is going. In all events, it should be clear that I love both the church and America. What may not be so clear is how these two loves relate or ought to relate. Like those on what is customarily regarded as the political and religious left, I am alarmed at recent American militaristic bellicosity and the present eclipse of such democratic ideals as the rule of law over the most powerful no less than the weakest among us. But like those on what is customarily regarded as the political and religious right, I believe Christianity has a role to play in public life, nationally and globally. In a book devoted to contradictions, I do not intend this to be another one. At the last, then, I turn to some overarching thoughts on baptism, patriotism, and being a Christian in public.

꙰꙰꙰꙰꙰꙰

Classically practiced, baptism is a political act. It is induction into a distinctive and determinative citizenship, citizenship in "a holy nation, God's own people" (1 Pet. 2:9). The people through which God chose to announce and witness God's reconciling and saving ways to the world

121

are the Jews. God acted in the history of ancient Israel to show who and what the true God among all gods is: the creator of the cosmos, the liberator from slavery, the giver of peace, the bringer of justice, the redeemer of a broken world. This God was known and sometimes recognized outside Israel, but especially and definitively *through* Israel, a people uniquely in relation (in covenant) with the true and living God. For the writers of the New Testament, Gentiles (non-Jews) outside this covenantal relationship were "aliens from the commonwealth of Israel, and strangers to the covenants of promise, having no hope and without God in the world" (Eph. 2:12). We Gentiles were men and women without a true home, bereft of citizenship and its responsibilities and privileges, really little more than bands of refugees wandering the face of the earth. In terms of identity and destiny, biblically speaking, there is no more fundamental divide than that between Jew and Gentile. This division breaks humanity into two fundamental parts. Citizenship in the commonwealth of Israel is that basic, that determinative. Race and gender and family have something to do with marking us and making us the persons we become. But nothing marks more deeply and more profoundly determines our destiny than whether we are Jews or Gentiles, citizens or aliens in "the commonwealth of Israel."

Can this gaping divide be bridged? Can alien Gentiles somehow become citizens? In Christian profession, Gentiles are called into covenantal relation with the God of Israel, the true and living God, through and by Jesus of Nazareth, himself a Jew and indeed the long-awaited Messiah. Drawing and adopting Gentiles into the commonwealth of Israel, Jesus Christ creates "one new humanity in place of the two" (Eph. 2:15). So for the baptized, nothing can be more basic or more significant than their baptism. In baptism, "There is no longer Jew or Greek, there is no longer slave or free, there is no longer male and female; for all of you are one in Christ Jesus" (Gal. 3:27–28). Just as immigrants or "aliens" from another country may be "naturalized" and become citizens of a new country, baptism "naturalizes" the Gentile, incorporates him or her into the body of the Jew Jesus Christ, and grants him or her citizenship in the "commonwealth of Israel." In the granting of this citizenship, baptism entails nothing less profound than entrance into a new creation, the assumption of a new humanity, a dying to the old self and its identity and a regeneration to a new self and identity (2 Cor. 5:17; Rom. 6:4). Nothing can more basically or comprehensively define the Christian than baptism. Membership in the worldwide body of Christ constitutes the Christian's highest loyalty, his or her central allegiance.

A few months after the events of September 11, 2001, a couple visited our church for some Sundays. They liked much of what they saw and heard, and were considering making our parish their worship home. In a visit with our priest, they voiced one major concern. American citizenship, they said, should be more prominently affirmed in the church's worship. Add more patriotic hymns, they suggested, and why not recite the pledge of allegiance during the liturgy? After pointing out that the corporate prayers of the people include intercession specifically for the United States, as well as its leaders of both federal and state government, our pastor counseled: "And we do say the pledge of allegiance—the church's pledge of allegiance. It's called the Nicene Creed." He was, as we Americans might say after the British, spot on. If we take seriously our baptisms and the Christian tradition, we are not first and foremost Americans, but Christians.

※※※※※※※

To say that the Christian's primary citizenship is in the church, the transnational body of Christ that points to his kingdom, his authority, is not to say that the Christian cannot simultaneously be the citizen of a secondary polity. The Christian can be, as many are, an American in good standing. I will go further. Patriotism, rightly understood, is something the Christian can wholeheartedly embrace.

The twentieth century was a fiery forge that showed the world that destruction and killing can occur on horrific scales, not only when traditional religions make calls to arms, but when nation-states do. The massively bloody buffoonery of World War I can be rationalized only to the degree it served nationalisms that were regarded as more basic than baptism and pitted Christian against Christian, as British vs. German (and so forth). Nazism and Soviet communism made no justificatory appeals to Judaism or Christianity, but rather erected their own substitute faiths and politico-religious rituals. These epochal events of the first half of the twentieth century drove two great democratic essayists, one American and one British, to close and penetrating reflection on authentic patriotism.

The American essayist, Randolph Bourne, wrote in the midst of World War I. His British counterpart, George Orwell, put pen to paper in the era of World War II. Though neither makes explicit reference to the word's etymology, both remember that *patriot* derives from the Latin for father, *pater.* The patriot is one who realizes and expresses gratitude to her fatherland. Much that has given her life and joy arises from the soil, the air and water, the forests and plains, the culture and customs of her homeland. Our biological mothers and fathers gift us with life. So, too, in less biological but still profound ways, do the countries that feed us long after we have left the mother's breast, that make us their citizens, that give us language to speak and stories to tell and songs to sing. We owe them much.

And notice how, exactly, we owe them. We owe them just as we owe our fathers and mothers. We owe them particularly. A child's love and loyalty is demonstrated not when she admires motherhood in the abstract or in principle, but when she embraces and appreciates the one, specific woman who gave her birth. So, too, as Orwell has it, patriotism is "devotion to a particular place and a particular way of life, one which one believes to be the best in the world but has no wish to force upon other people."[1] For me, my parents were and are the best parents in the world. But I am not aggressive or exclusive in this claim. If you believe your parents are the best in the world, I can grant you that without dishonoring my own parents. I have "no wish to force upon other people" the conviction that my mother is the greatest of all mothers. The very nature of love for parents not only allows but demands that we each embrace our particular parents above all others. None of us chooses our parents. The lucky among us indeed have fine and loving parents. For good and ill, we all owe our own parents for much of what we are, for the very fact that we are. We love them accordingly, and of course this love does not entail that we approve everything they do or even all that they are. You can disapprove of your father's divorce and yet have him remain your beloved father. You can regret your mother's alcoholism and still claim her wholeheartedly as your mother.

Likewise, says Bourne in relation to patriotism, "We are part of a country for better or for worse. We have arrived in it through the operation of physiological laws, and not in any way through our own choice. By the time we have reached what are called years of discretion, its influences have molded our habits, our values, our ways of thinking, so that however aware we may become, we never really lose the stamp of our civilization, or could become the child of another country."[2] In Orwell's words, your country is yours—"Good or evil, it is yours, you belong to it, and this side of the grave you will never get away from the marks it has given you."[3]

Clearly patriotism—as the very word itself suggests—operates on the same logic as that of love for parents. It is "essentially noncompetitive" and does not seek "competitive prestige," in that it allows citizens of other countries to be loyal patriots of their own homes.[4] It does not live or die by a succession of loyalty tests that endorse (or resist) its current government's latest actions. The patriot may disagree with or protest her country's actions without ceasing to be a patriot. (In fact, we would not say that an adult child who passively stood by and let his parents undertake a destructive course of action was as loving as the one who actively worked to steer his parents off a disastrous path.) Patriotism, as such, is focused inward (toward one's own country) and not outward (in reaction to another country). It is "intensive and not belligerent," defensive rather than aggressive.[5]

In this light, flag-waving may be not the height of patriotism but its cheapening and trivialization. As Bourne notes, "The flag is primarily the banner of war." Intimately connected with military achievement and memory, it is a symbol of the state's will to power, to "prestige and expansion." As such, the flag "represents the country not in its intensive life, but in its far-flung challenge to the world."[6] Compared to serious citizenship, flag-waving is easy. It can be a way of pretending to costly loyalty without making any commitment more strenuous than house decoration.

Perhaps Bourne presses the matter a bit too far. There is, after all, such a thing as a defensive war. Though flag-waving in and of itself does not prove patriotism (and is certainly not the essence of patriotism), the flag can represent a country's goods intensively and nonbelligerently. That is why flags can fly peaceably beside one another, as on neighboring sides of the Canadian-U.S. border, or in the plaza of the headquarters of the United Nations. Overall, however, Bourne is right to remind us of the flag's militaristic provenance, and to be wary of identifying war with patriotism. War, with its terrible demands to kill and die, can exact sacrifices that test the mettle of a citizen's patriotism and maturity. But war also can create conditions in which citizens do not rise to adult responsibilities so much as they abdicate those responsibilities and revert to a childlike state. As Bourne writes, a people at war can "become in the most literal sense obedient, respectful, trustful children again, full of that naive faith in the all-wisdom and all-power of the adult who takes care of them, imposes his mild but necessary rule on them and in whom they lose their responsibility and anxieties."[7] It is not patriotism simply to trust whatever the government says, or to approve every warlike passion sweeping one's nation. True patriotism, and what we have earlier called a democracy for grown-ups, demands the shouldering of responsibilities and anxieties. It will on frequent occasion entail loyal resistance and will always beware of war's seductions toward a childish and savage primal unity.[8]

※※※※※※

In sum, asked how I might suppose a baptized Christian could also be an American patriot, I would reply: in the same way one is a baptized Christian and strives to be a loyal mature son to his elders. The commitment of baptism is comprehensive or basic, and when push comes to shove, overrules particular commitments to one's parents and one's nation. In the best of cases, baptism and Christian practice will shape, empower, and restrain the lesser (while still profound) commitments of parent love and patriotism. Tensions between these multiple commitments will then be mild. At times, however, there may well be great and painful tension: as with the adult child who confesses her parents are guilty of theft or another crime, or when the patriot concludes his country has been wrong or even criminal in its policy and calls it to account. Such tensions can never be welcome but should also never be a surprise to the mature democrat, who faces and admits the inevitability of the tragic in a world of finite and broken creatures.

While erring but still loved parents and countries are imaginable to most today, many others will take exception to the idea (let alone the reality) of baptism as a comprehensive and public commitment. Throughout modernity, religion has been regarded like sex: something fine to enjoy in private, but never to be done in public. This categorization and relegation of faith to the private and individual has been accepted by many modern Christians. It showed up for a period quite starkly in the custom of "private baptisms." Here families would convene on a Sunday afternoon, or some other time outside the community's gathered worship, and see a child baptized "privately" amid its small party of relatives. Such a private baptism is depicted in Francis Ford Coppola's *The Godfather.* Michael Corleone has assigned hit jobs on several of his mafia enemies. These killings are carried out as Michael and his relatives gather in a church to see the newest member of their family baptized. Coppola intercuts scenes of the baptism (the priest pouring water on the baby, the adoring family reciting parts of the ritual in Latin) with the assassinations (a man on a massage table shot in the eye, another gunned down on the steps of a courthouse). The compartmentalization and, indeed, the emasculation of the Corleones' faith is here captured brilliantly and stunningly. The private baptism has nothing to do with the Corleones' brutal livelihood, no sway over "real life." It entails no accountability outside the sentimentalized, insulated confines of a small circle of relatives.

Though typical instances of private baptism are not so glaringly out of joint with Christian practice as the Corleones', theologians and the churches have recently recognized the patent incongruity and inappropriateness of baptism as a private or secluded event. The very word for corporate worship, *liturgy,* derives from the Latin for "the work of the people," or public labor. In the Roman world of the early Christians, a liturgy (a work of the people) was underway when a bridge or a road was built for common use. As the above cited passages from 1 Peter and Ephesians indicate, the biblical Christians understood the church as a "nation," a body of citizens—in short, as itself a kind of public. To be baptized was to be inducted into this public, with the appropriate privileges and responsibilities of citizenship in that public. Baptism meant accepting and declaring Christ as Lord above all other lords, including Caesar, who would have himself called Lord.

Thus the church itself is a kind of public, composed of citizens who are baptized into the (social and spiritual) body of Christ, who strive for the common good in the form of witnessing to the kingdom of God Christ has inaugurated and will one day bring to its consummation or fullness. What then becomes clear is not that Christian faith and life is apolitical, private, and confined to the feelings of individuals, but that Christians are members of a public named church. A mark of any public is that it is known and recognized as a people, a public, both by itself and by those outside it. There can be no Americans apart from a public known as America; in the same way, there are no Christians apart from the public known as church. Baptism means more than this, but it means no less.

⚅⚅⚅⚅⚅⚅

If the church is enacted and treated as a public, and Christianity not merely or primarily as a private but a public faith, we are definitely being truer to the biblical and classical understandings of the faith. Are we then also and necessarily committed to a theocratic nation-state or, in this particular case, to a Christian America? On the contrary, if we are committed to the church as a public, we will be wary of any other publics or public bodies that would assume the church's mission. Something like a Christian America (or any other Christian state) might be needed if the faith and the church were only a matter for "private life." But if the church is itself a public, it performs its own public work. Yearning and striving for a Christian America does not serve the church. Instead, it presumes on the church's mission and dismisses the church as itself a public.[9]

Then should the church itself dream of forming its own armies, levying taxation, and promulgating laws for everyone within its territories? To think so is to imagine the church as the sort of public it is not. Lawmaking and a monopoly on legitimatized violence are marks of the public that is the nation-state. The church is a different sort of public, built on and living out of the cross of Christ. It is a public marked by love rather than coercion, service rather than mastery. It grows not by might but by persuasion in the power of the Holy Spirit. It resists and fights evil by means of its members' fortitude, patience, and sacrifice. Only so can it be true to the cross of Christ that gives it being and lends it a distinctive public shape. Confusing the church's mission with any nation-state's purpose misconstrues the Christian faith and distorts the face of Christ before a watching world. It makes the cross bearer into a sword bearer, the Prince of Peace into a Machiavellian politico, the Lord of all nations into the jealous advocate of a single nation.

So baptism and its entailments can bring a citizen of the public called church into tension with citizenship in a public known as the nation-state. There will be occasions when Christians as members of the church refuse to fight in certain wars, or stand up against particular injustices, of the nation-state. But citizenship in the Christian public does not exclude citizenship in other publics, including the nation-state. A public is not a physical space so much as it is a people who share a common good and move about all variety of physical spaces.[10] Moreover, persons can belong to more than one public, and even belong to more than one public at once. At a meeting of Illinoisans for Cleaner Air, I can simultaneously be both a member of the public that is the state Illinois and a member of the larger public that is the nation-state America, which determines minimal air standards in Wisconsin no less than Illinois. Similarly, the Christian's primary and most comprehensive allegiance is determined by her baptism, but that does not prevent her enthusiastic devotion to her parents, to the wonders of American music, to the breathtakingly varied topography of her home country, to service on the town council, and to the duties of American citizenship.[11]

Why should Christians care about and belong to more than one public? In our own terms, we should do so because we are called to care for neighbors. In the story usually referred to as the parable of the Good Samaritan, Jesus made it clear that neighbors are quite simply the persons at hand—including our enemies. They are the people we happen to live with and alongside. They are the people in need whom we might help. Their welfare is our concern. In the modern world, with its transportation and communication capabilities that interconnect and overlap peoples' welfare across the globe, love of neighbor demands conscientious participation in numerous publics, including that of the nation-state.

In this light, as we argued in an earlier chapter, one of the worst temptations facing contemporary Christians is to scapegoat or demonize the "others" outside our favorite Christian circles. Anger can be a motivating and galvanizing energy, especially in an urgent age of so many divisions and of overwhelming mass-media and Internet communication, a setting in which the loudest voice appears to get the most attention. But if professing Christians define ourselves by our enemies and see ourselves fundamentally in an antagonistic relationship with those who are different and with whom we disagree, we betray that we have not understood the parable of the Good Samaritan—let alone the cross and resurrection of Jesus Christ. Because God is the creator of all and Christ comes to redeem all, Karl Barth is right to say, "It is better not to describe [the Christian] as a warrior. If he is in his right senses, he will not think of himself as such." The Christian (and the church) disagrees and refuses to conform to the world "not in opposition to any other men, but on behalf of all other men, as one who has to show them the liberation which has already taken place [in Christ's death and resurrection]." Truly, even the *militia Christi,* the "soldiers" of the church militant, "will not really consist in conflict against others, but *decisively in conflict against oneself,* and in the fact that one is assailed, and in some way has to suffer, and to accept suffering, at the hands of others."[12] This is Christian discipleship for grown-ups, entailing skills and dispositions similar to those required by democracy for grown-ups.

The simply grasped (but often demandingly honored) responsibility of neighbor love is more than enough to propel Christians into publics in addition to the church. But we should be clear that Christians are called to multiple publics not only to help others—that would be irksome and tiresome to the others we think we can relate to only as our dependents. We are called to multiple publics not merely to help but to be helped. Or, to take it away from potentially patronizing language altogether, we are called to multiple publics because God and God's kingdom are bigger and beyond any single public, including the public that is the church.

The church is an invention of God, not God the invention of the church. By Christian profession, following our Jewish elder siblings, God is the inventor and sustainer of the universe and of all history. Accordingly, God is at work not only in the church as a public, but— one way or another—throughout all God's creation, across all history, in all publics. Christians claim that God has acted decisively in Christ, and that through the work of Christ we best discern the world's true shape and actual destiny. So Christ provides Christians a kind of hermeneutics through which we read and interpret the world. The Bible, then, is a text providing the decisive patterns through which we read the world, while it is not the sole or exclusive "text" we read. Since God and Christ are always greater than any of our readings, Christians constantly stand to learn and be enriched by texts outside the church's sacred library, by publics other than the church. The examples, both small and large, are unpredictable and endless. Native Americans and the agnostic leaders of the European Enlightenment have helped the church better understand and practice freedom of religion and democracy. Christian architecture, to God's glory, has borrowed from pagan architecture, and Christian celebration from pagan holidays. Non-Christian musics have vitalized and renewed Christian hymnody. Put constructively, signs of the kingdom of the God met in Christ can be found in various wonders, varieties, quandaries, and mysteries across creation and in all cultures. Put negatively, the Christian who closes himself off to these signs and works of God beyond the public that is the church makes God smaller than the church, manageable by the church, and so makes an idol of the church. And idolatry is a betrayal of baptism.

❧❧❧❧❧❧

The theological and roughly systematic remarks of this concluding chapter bring to the surface the convictions undergirding all the preceding chapters. I surface them because some (maybe even many) readers will have wondered, as they patiently followed my arguments, if there is any coherent framework for my presumption that Christians, precisely as Christians, have something to say to and about America. I surface them at the *end* of the book because, if I have been at all successful, the claims and suggestions of the earlier chapters (1) will have made some sense on their own and (2) will have shown in practice what I am in this final chapter trying to say in theory or principle.

Johnny Cash never talked the way I have talked in these pages. He was a poet and not a critic. He was a genius of the people and not simply of the people. In his own way he surely dealt with the themes of lonesomeness and community, holiness and hedonism, tradition and progress, guilt and innocence, and peace and violence. I want to believe that, were he alive, he might read these pages with some intrigue and a good deal of agreement. But of this much I am certain: the man was a Christian, and he was an American. And so am I.

Notes

INTRODUCTION

1. Ron Suskind, *The One-Percent Doctrine: Deep Inside America's Pursuit of Its Enemies since 9/11* (New York: Simon & Schuster, 2006), 336–37.

2. See Kevin Phillips, *American Theocracy: The Peril of Politics of Radical Religion, Oil, and Borrowed Money in the 21st Century* (New York: Viking, 2006), 188 and 233.

3. In some sense the church wants to call the world's contradictions to the world's attention, in ways that the church, as the unique social witness to the good news of redemption in Christ, is alone equipped to do. In this regard there is promise and grace in contradiction. As Karl Barth comments, "[The church] exists . . . to set up in the world a new sign which is radically dissimilar to [the world's] own manner and which contradicts it in a way that is full of promise. In all its creaturely impotence and human corruption, [the church] is required to do this." See Barth, *Church Dogmatics* IV/3.2, ed. G. W. Bromiley and T. F. Torrance, trans. G. W. Bromiley (Edinburgh: T. & T. Clark, 1962), 779.

4. This 1990 census figure is cited in Cecelia Tichi, ed., *Reading Country Music: Steel Guitars, Opry Stars, and Honky Tonk Bars* (Durham, NC: Duke University Press, 1998), 202–3.

5. These January 2005 figures are cited in Chris Willman, *Rednecks and Bluenecks: The Politics of Country Music* (New York: New Press, 2005), 6.

6. Bill C. Malone, *Don't Get above Your Raisin': Country Music and the Southern Working Class* (Urbana and Chicago: University of Illinois Press, 2002), 252 and 14.

7. On the Nashville Fan Fair and the workings of country music celebrity, see Laurence Leamer, *Three Chords and the Truth: Behind the Scenes with Those Who Make and Shape Country Music* (New York: Harper Paperbacks, 1997).

8. They are scarce but by no means entirely absent, as Pamela E. Foster's 378-page compendium demonstrates. See her *My Country: The African Diaspora's Country Music Heritage* (Nashville: Pamela E. Foster, 1998).

133

9. See Michael Streissguth, *Johnny Cash: The Biography* (Cambridge, MA: Da Capo Press, 2006), xiv and 123.

10. Steve Turner, *The Man Called Cash: The Authorized Biography* (Nashville: W Publishing Group, 2004), 139 and 227.

11. Ibid., 86.

12. *Ring of Fire: The Johnny Cash Reader,* ed. Michael Streissguth (Cambridge, MA: Da Capo Press, 2002), 99.

13. Family and friends surviving Cash testify that he was deeply disturbed by the U.S. action on Iraq in 1993, and positively against that of 2003. See for instance Turner, *The Man Called Cash,* 246, and Willman, *Rednecks and Bluenecks,* 251.

14. Streissguth, *Ring of Fire,* 119.

15. Bob Dylan, *Chronicles: Volume One* (New York: Simon & Schuster, 2004), 217.

16. The brilliance of "Folsom Prison Blues" is somewhat dimmed by the fact that it was in part plagiarized from an earlier source. See Michael Streissguth, *Johnny Cash at Folsom Prison: The Making of a Masterpiece* (Cambridge, MA: Da Capo Press, 2004), 20–22.

17. "A Boy Named Sue" was, in chart-topping terms, the biggest hit of Cash's career, but was written by Shel Silverstein and is usually not named among Cash's greatest songs. Nonetheless, his craggy spoken delivery of lines such as "we kicked and we gouged / in the mud, and the blood, and the beer" is captivating and unforgettable, lifting the song above mere and ephemeral cleverness. Hear it at Johnny Cash, *At San Quentin (The Complete 1969 Concert),* Columbia/Legacy CK 66017.

CHAPTER 1: AMERICA'S SOUTHERN ACCENT

1. Tom Petty, "Southern Accents" (Gone Gator Music); hear it at Johnny Cash, *Unchained,* American 314 586 791-2.

2. Neither this metaphor nor any other single metaphor can capture all the rich facets of Whitman's democracy. The South enchanted Whitman. He was not concerned to pit himself or his work monolithically against it. And of course the Emersonian elements in Whitman's work ("I celebrate myself," etc.) point up the pronounced quasi-gnostic individualism quite pervasive and powerful in northern or "Yankee" democracy. For Whitman's attitudes on these matters, see David S. Reynolds, *Walt Whitman's America: A Cultural Biography* (New York: Vintage Books, 1995).

3. All citations from *Leaves of Grass* come from the Penguin Books 2005 rendition of the first, 1855 edition (New York, introduction by Harold Bloom).

4. The Mayflower Compact opens by declaring that the pilgrims "Covenant and Combine ourselves together in a Civil Body Politic" (William Bradford, *Of Plymouth Plantation: 1620–1647,* ed. Samuel Eliot Morison [New York: Modern Library, 1952], 76).

5. W. J. Cash, *The Mind of the South* (New York: Vintage Books, 1941, 1991), 32.

6. For a compelling account of American Christian individualism, from the Puritans to early and later revivalism, see John W. Wright, *Telling God's Story: Nar-*

rative Preaching for Christian Formation (Downers Grove, IL: InterVarsity Press, 2007), 47–76.

7. Wright, *Telling God's Story,* comments on the dynamic of revivalistic Christian movements which begin with a concentration on the poor and dispossessed but gravitate over time toward the middle and upper classes. "What seems to happen is a process of what Donald Dayton has called 'embourgoisement.' With no ecclesiology committed to the gospel teachings of Jesus or the Pauline or Jamesian ecclesial formation, the covenant of grace, which often begins embracing the poor, tends to become upwardly mobile. Because salvation is solely individual, the church moves toward the wealthy and powerful within society as the preferred market for the individual narrative of salvation. By reaching the influential, it is hoped that covenant of grace will envelop more and more people through the resources and influence that power and wealth possess" (72).

8. Tom T. Hall, "Me and Jesus" (Mercury Nashville); hear it at Tom T. Hall, *The Definitive Collection,* Hip-o 80005943-02.

9. A recent, richly detailed, and brilliant examination of the nineteenth-century revivals is Ted A. Smith, *The New Measures: A Theological History of Democratic Practice* (New York: Cambridge University Press, 2007). Smith unearths with great nuance how revivalism has contributed profoundly to current American and American Christian obsession with celebrity, novelty, choice, technique, spiritual kitschiness, and instrumentalized faith. At the same time, he is not simply dismissive of revivalism. He submits himself to a "critical resignation" to "a culture that is neither other, or whole, or ideal" (23) and strives neither to "damn" or "reject," nor to "celebrate" or "affirm" his subjects of study (12, 13). Rather, Smith attempts attentively and subtly to scrutinize the practices of revivalism and "break them open so that they might testify to a hope against their hope" (13), to discern how the grace of God has worked both "in" and "in spite of" revivialistic schemes, events, and testimony. This critical resignation and "in/in spite of" dialectical refusal of decisive evaluation enables Smith to provide a salutarily complicated, illuminating, and indispensable account of revivalistic practices now over a century old. However, it leaves us little by way of criteria, method, or practical orientation with which to discern and judge current revivalism. More to the point, it does not readily enable (and perhaps it disables) imagination of how specific current revivalistic practices and acts of revivalists might be (at least partially) corrected so that God might work more "in" them than "in spite of them."

10. H. Richard Niebuhr, *The Kingdom of God in America* (New York: Harper & Row, 1937), 181; for the entirety of Niebuhr's illuminating discussion of American revivalism, see 179–84.

11. One of the classic short stories of the twentieth century—Flannery O'Connor's "Revelation"—actually concludes with a great democratic parade, a vision of souls of various classes and races marching heavenwardly "into the starry field and shouting hallelujah." O'Connor's Roman Catholicism enabled her to see beyond the (Protestant) revivalistic democracy of her southern homeland to democracy as parade. "Revelation" is included in Flannery O'Connor, *The Complete Stories* (New York: Farrar, Straus & Giroux, 1971), 488–509; quotation 509.

12. See, for example, Thomas Frank, *What's the Matter with Kansas? How Conservatives Won the Heart of America* (New York: Metropolitan Books, 2004).

13. The Southern Strategy has been documented by a growing literature. My account draws mainly on Peter Applebome, *Dixie Rising: How the South Is Shaping American Values, Politics, and Culture* (New York: Times Books, 1996); Steve Jarding and Dave "Mudcat" Saunders, *Foxes in the Henhouse: How the Republicans Stole the South and the Heartland* (New York: Touchstone, 2006); Lisa McGirr, *Suburban Warriors: The Origins of the New American Right* (Princeton, NJ: Princeton University Press, 2001); and Kevin Phillips, *American Theocracy: The Peril and Politics of Radical Religion, Oil, and Borrowed Money in the 21st Century* (New York: Viking, 2006).

14. Introduction to Cash, *The Mind of the South*, viii.

15. Ibid., 10.

16. Quoted in Bill C. Malone, *Don't Get above Your Raisin': Country Music and the Southern Working Class* (Urbana and Chicago: University of Illinois Press, 2002), 229. I alter the spelling as it appears in Malone's text, from "pore" to "poor."

17. Virginia, North Carolina, South Carolina, Georgia, Florida, Tennessee, Arkansas, Alabama, Mississippi, Louisiana, and Texas.

18. Applebome, *Dixie Rising*, 8.

19. Ibid., 9.

20. The Marxist label was applied to Wallace by *The National Review.* Quoted in Christopher Lasch, *The True and Only Heaven: Progress and Its Critics* (New York: W. W. Norton & Co., 1991), 505.

21. Tipping the hand on racial allusions were statements by Ronald Reagan pitting "law and order" against an ever encroaching "jungle" threatening to overrun civilized society. See McGirr, *Suburban Warriors,* 204.

22. For an extended discussion of this approach to culture, see Rodney Clapp, *A Peculiar People: The Church as Culture in a Post-Christian Society* (Downers Grove, IL: InterVarsity Press, 1996), 58–75.

23. I say culture "in its most comprehensive forms" because there are many smaller or "sub" cultures that define lesser, more limited parts of our identities. So we can sensibly speak of a "culture of hip-hop" or a "culture of Civil War reenactors" or a "culture of country club golfers" without assuming these cultures so fundamentally and completely define their adherents as do broader, more fundamental manifestations of culture such as Russia, modernity, or Christianity.

24. I say that allegiance reveals one's "real worship," but this worship is not necessarily true. True worship, as the Decalogue indicates, bows only to the God of Israel, met in Christ. The possibility of real yet false worship is why Judaism and Christianity have idolatry as a category. Idolatry is making a religion or ultimate concern of something or someone that should not be an object of worship, of unsurpassed loyalty and trust. Since cultures are all about organizing, interpreting, and lending significance to our lives, profound or comprehensive cultures easily gravitate toward being de facto religions (idolatrous, perhaps, but religions nonetheless).

25. Paul Tillich, *Theology of Culture,* ed. Robert C. Kimball (New York: Oxford

University Press, 1959), 42. By citing Tillich's famous and helpful formulation I am not endorsing Tillich's overall theology of culture, and certainly not his method of correlation, which approached supposedly universal and abstract philosophical affirmations of secular culture and made them (logically and theologically) prior to the story of Israel and Jesus Christ in discerning and determining the course of history. The definitive and essential account of a theology of culture that accepts Tillich as "a point of departure" but insists on the centrality of the "Gospel Story" is James Wm. McClendon Jr., *Witness: Systematic Theology,* vol. 3 (Nashville: Abingdon Press, 2000). As McClendon writes, "If we use his old Greek categories [of form and substance], Paul Tillich was right when he claimed that religion is the substance of culture, culture is the form of religion. He was wrong, though, to assume in nineteenth-century fashion that in any given place there will be only one religion, only one culture. It has steadily become more clear that in his day as now there were many cultures, many religions, many 'gods' (1 Cor. 8:5)." Furthermore, and *pace* Tillich, none of the secular "episodes so fully discloses the gospel, even in its time and place, as to become a standard measure, a measure [instead] given for good and all in Jesus Christ." See 57 and 97.

26. Cash, *The Mind of the South,* 38.

27. I should note that American popular culture is of course not simply its music. Television, films, and video-game production are hugely important practices of American popular culture, and these industries are based primarily in California and New York City. I do not at all want to insist American popular culture—let alone culture in general—is merely southern. I am saying southern influence of American popular culture as a whole is remarkable and widespread. The southern accent resounds well beyond the borders of the old Confederacy. It is worth remarking that in the 1860s and 1870s, mining, the construction of the transcontinental railroads, and finally cattle drives drew many southerners into Montana and Wyoming. Missouri and Texas were the second and third ranking states sending migrants into California in the 1920s, with more from there and the border state of Oklahoma escaping the Dust Bowl to the Golden State in the thirties. In light of these migrations Kevin Phillips remarks that the West, in cultural and religious terms, became a kind of adjunct of the South. See *American Theocracy,* 167. Also see James N. Gregory, *American Exodus: The Dust Bowl Migration and Okie Culture in California* (New York: Oxford University Press, 1991).

28. Theological and southern grounds for democracy as parade also come together in Flannery O'Connor. See note 11.

29. Steve Turner, *The Man Called Cash: The Authorized Biography* (Nashville: W Publishing Group, 2004), 156.

30. Tom Waits, "Down There by the Train" (Jalma Music Inc.); hear it at *Johnny Cash: American Recordings,* American 9 45520-2.

31. Turner, *The Man Called Cash,* 222.

CHAPTER 2: LONESOMENESS AND COMMUNITY

1. In her deeply sympathetic—no, empathetic—book, Miles comments that her hill-country neighbors are "folks so little given to retrospection that they can hardly

discover what are their own inmost thoughts, much less give them expression." *The Spirit of the Mountains* (Knoxville: University of Tennessee Press, 1975 edition), 138.

2. Ibid., 17.

3. Ibid., 18 and 19.

4. Ibid., 153.

5. Ibid., 128–29.

6. Ibid., 131.

7. Country singer Webb Pierce remarks, "One of the things is you sing about things they [listeners] think about the most, but don't talk about. That becomes an emotional outlet for the people, and they feel they have a friend in the song" (Cited in Tex Sample, *White Soul: Country Music, the Church, and Working Americans* [Nashville: Abingdon Press, 1996], 74).

8. *Bob Dylan: No Direction Home,* DVD, directed by Martin Scorcese (Los Angeles: Paramount Home Entertainment, 2005).

9. Of course, especially for Pentecostal country folk, worship was another medium for vigorous emotionalism. Here, too, however, music was the main medium allowing the entire congregation (not just the preacher) to freely express themselves.

10. Hank Williams, "I'm So Lonesome I Could Cry" (Acuff-Rose Music, Inc./Hiriam Music); hear it at Hank Williams, *24 of Hank Williams' Greatest Hits,* Mercury Nashville 823 293-2.

11. Hank Williams, "Nobody's Lonesome for Me" (Acuff-Rose Music, Inc./Hiriam Music); hear it at Hank Williams Sr., *24 Greatest Hits, Vol. 2*, Mercury Nashville 823 294-2.

12. It is a measure of Williams's genius as a lyricist that Leonard Cohen, perhaps the finest popular poet/songwriter of our day, places Williams 100 levels above himself in the North American "Tower of Song." (Hear Cohen's song by that name, in any of its many recorded versions.)

13. Colin Escott with George Merritt and William MacEwan, *Hank Williams: The Biography* (New York and Boston: Little, Brown & Co., 2004), 124–25.

14. Cash was also skilled in anthropomorphization, as evidenced by such standouts as "I Still Miss Someone," "Big River," "You Wild Colorado," and his wistfully stark performance of Kris Kristofferson's "Sunday Morning Coming Down."

15. Mark Zwonitzer with Charles Hirshberg, *Will You Miss Me When I'm Gone? The Carter Family and Their Legacy in American Music* (New York: Simon & Schuster, 2002), 137–38.

16. Johnny Cash, "Big River" (no publisher provided); Johnny Cash, *The Sun Years,* Sun/Rhino R2 70950.

17. Angela Y. Davis, *Blues Legacies and Black Feminism: Gertrude "Ma" Rainey, Bessie Smith, and Billie Holiday* (New York: Pantheon Books, 1998), 44–45.

18. Ibid., 19, 67, 69.

19. Bill C. Malone, *Don't Get above Your Raisin': Country Music and the Southern Working Class* (Urbana and Chicago: University of Illinois Press, 2002), 119.

20. Jimmie Rodgers, "Blue Yodel No. 1 (T for Texas)." Jimmie Rodgers, *RCA Country Legends,* iTunes download, no further information provided.

21. See Robert D. Putnam, *Bowling Alone: The Collapse and Revival of American Community* (New York: Simon & Schuster, 2000); Robert N. Bellah et al., *Habits of the Heart* (Berkeley: University of California Press, 1985); and Robert Putnam, "You Gotta Have Friends: A Study Finds that Americans Are Getting Lonelier," *Time,* July 3, 2006, 36.

22. Cited in Barry Alan Shain, *The Myth of American Individualism: The Protestant Origins of American Political Thought* (Princeton, NJ: Princeton University Press, 1994), 56.

23. Quoted in ibid., 39.

24. But only apparently. We can imagine ourselves self-sufficient via means of our technologies only so long as we forget that others invent, develop, and maintain our increasingly complex tools. The complexity of our tools in fact makes us less self-sufficient than the nineteenth-century farmers who could repair wagons, harnesses, and other tools of the trade by themselves, with materials at hand. By contrast, few of us can build or repair our own computers. Furthermore, advanced technology is more centralized and interconnected than simpler technology. Massive infrastructure means that electrical plant failures in one state may affect a region of several states, so that the lights go out from Pittsburgh to New York City. The oil lantern, by contrast, burns in Pennsylvania even if the fuel supply is interrupted in New York.

25. Lisa McGirr, *Suburban Warriors: The Origins of the New American Right* (Princeton, NJ: Princeton University Press, 2001), 26.

26. Ibid., 13–14.

27. Ibid., 9.

28. Ibid., 38–39.

29. Of course, the comparative affluence of wide swaths of Americans also allows even many poorer Americans to own televisions, cell phones, laptops, and other technologies that enable and enhance individualism by piecing together "virtual community." Without the widespread availability of such devices, lonesomeness and the breakdown of culture and community would appear more starkly and probably exacerbate class tensions far above their current levels.

30. For principled wrestling with the acute contradictions across sectors of American conservatism, and a serious argument that many of those who call themselves conservative in the current Republican Party are not conservative in any deep or traditional sense, see Andrew Sullivan, *The Conservative Soul: How We Lost It, How to Get It Back* (New York: HarperCollins, 2006).

31. Cited in Richard T. Hughes, *Myths America Lives By* (Urbana and Chicago: University of Illinois Press, 2003), 155–56.

32. For "Okie Culture," see James N. Gregory, *American Exodus: The Dust Bowl Migration and Okie Culture in California* (New York: Oxford University Press, 1991), 142–51; and for "proprietary democracy," see Christopher Lasch, *The True and Only Heaven: Progress and Its Critics* (New York: W. W. Norton & Co., 1991), 14–17.

33. Martin Luther King Jr., *A Testament of Hope: The Essential Writings of Martin Luther King, Jr.,* ed. James M. Washington (San Francisco: Harper & Row, 1986), 626.

34. Cornel West, *Prophetic Fragments* (Grand Rapids: Eerdmans/Trenton, NJ: Africa World Press, 1988), 165. In the penultimate sentence from this quotation, I substitute the term "comic" where West uses the term "utopian." I do so for ease of communication, to avoid introducing a third technical term ("utopian") into discussion at this point. In his original context, West focuses mainly on the tragic and the comic, and nuances that discussion with a description of the "utopian." My adaptation obviously loses this nuancing, but remains faithful to the overall thrust of his astute comments on tragedy and comedy.

35. I refer here to *American Recordings; Unchained; American III; American IV;* and *American V.*

36. Trent Reznor, "Hurt" (Leaving Hope Music/TVT Music, Inc.); on Johnny Cash, *American IV: The Man Comes Around,* American 440 063 339 2. What does it say that this song is a cover of a song written by a gothic rocker named Trent Reznor, someone emblematic in many eyes of the darkest and worst of popular culture? At least it says that Cash can see unsentimental honesty wherever it manifests itself. It says that truth can sometimes most readily be declared from the margins rather than from the center of power and comfort, often eager to cosmeticize the world it thinks it has created and controls.

37. John R. Cash, "The Man Comes Around" (Song of Cash Music, Inc.); on Johnny Cash, *American IV.*

CHAPTER 3: HOLINESS AND HEDONISM

1. By my quick and dirty count, Cash was a generous "tither" indeed. Totaling tracks on his Sun, Columbia, Mercury, and American albums (plus *Personal File* [Columbia/Legacy 82796 94265 2]—excluding hits and other compilation albums—Cash waxed 964 songs, with 235 (24 percent) explicitly religious. On Cash's ten-percent pledge, see Steve Turner, *The Man Called Cash: The Authorized Biography* (Nashville: W Publishing Group, 2004), 76. For a web discography including track listings, see www.luma-electronic.cz/lp/c/Cash/cash2.htm. Accessed June 1, 2007.

2. T. J. Arnall, "Cocaine Blues" (no further information provided); from Johnny Cash, *At Folsom Prison,* Columbia/Legacy CK 65955.

3. See Bill C. Malone, *Don't Get above Your Raisin': Country Music and the Southern Working Class* (Urbana and Chicago: University of Illinois Press, 2002), 106.

4. "Red Nightgown Blues," recorded in 1932, is found on volume 2 (*The First Time I Met the Blues)* of the excellent roots music collection *When the Sun Goes Down* (Bluebird 09026-63978-2).

5. On Jerry Lee's ambivalence, see Nick Tosches, *Country: The Twisted Roots of Rock 'n' Roll* (New York: Da Capo Press, 1996), 66–68; and Turner, *The Man Called Cash,* 76.

6. This well before rock musicians took to performative destruction of their guitars. Johnny Cash initiated what would become the rock tradition of trashing hotel rooms. Before so much of the ethos and music was "only rock and roll," it was country. "Broadminded," by Ira Louvin and Charles Louvin (no further publishing infor-

mation provided), can be heard on *When I Stop Dreaming: The Best of the Louvin Brothers,* Razor & Tie, RE 2068.

7. See the outstanding account of the Louvin Brothers in Nicholas Dawidoff, *In the Country of Country: People and Places in American Music* (New York: Pantheon Books, 1997), 133–47.

8. Gordon L. Anderson, *Philosophy of the United States: Life, Liberty, and the Pursuit of Happiness* (St. Paul, MN: Paragon House, 2004), 70.

9. Thus the Trinity, a keystone doctrine for any remotely orthodox Christian theology, was anathema to the deists. The mystery of Father, Son, and Holy Spirit as three and yet no less one aggrieved humanistic rationalism. Profound consequences follow. If Father, Son, and Holy Spirit are simply three, Christians are polytheists and decisively depart the monotheism of their Jewish mother faith. If Christ the Son is not divine (as well as fully human), then he cannot be the incarnate Savior of creation. Deists, such as Thomas Jefferson, typically opted for retaining monotheism and demoting Jesus Christ to a great but not more than human moral sage.

10. Avery Cardinal Dulles, "The Deist Minimum," *First Things,* January 2005, 28. For a helpful and concise summary of religious attitudes in eighteenth-century America, see also Michael Bailey, *Prism,* January/February 2006, 19–21.

11. See Dulles, "The Deist Minimum," 27. Similarly, French philosopher Jean-Jacques Rousseau affirmed a kind of deistic civil religion because he could not imagine the sustenance of the social contract without belief in "a mighty, intelligent, beneficent deity" and a life to come with rewards for the just and punishment for the wicked (ibid., 29).

12. For more on how the "God" of American civil religion is explicitly not the God of historic Christianity, see Rodney Clapp, "Hollow Pledge: The Problem with 'under God,'" *Christian Century,* November 16, 2004, 30–33.

13. Richard T. Hughes, *Myths America Lives By* (Urbana and Chicago: University of Illinois Press, 2003), 54–56.

14. Quoted in W. J. Cash, *The Mind of the South* (New York: Vintage Books, 1941, 1991), 80. See also Grant Wacker and Todd Shy, "Christians and the Civil War," *Christian Century,* May 30, 2006, 28–37. For a sense of how the southern defense of slavery was Christianized, with the challenge of slavery framed as a decisive attack on the authority of Scripture, see Willard M. Swartley, *Slavery, Sabbath, War, and Women: Case Issues in Biblical Interpretation* (Scottdale, PA: Herald Press, 1983), 31–64. For an extensive detail and overview, see Elizabeth Fox-Genovese and Eugene D. Genovese, *The Mind of the Master Class: History and Faith in the Southern Slaveholders' Worldview* (Cambridge: Cambridge University Press, 2005), 409–646.

15. The standard histories of evangelicalism in twentieth-century America are George M. Marsden, *Fundamentalism and American Culture,* 2nd ed. (New York: Oxford University Press, 2006); and Marsden, *Reforming Fundamentalism: Fuller Seminary and the New Evangelicalism* (Grand Rapids: Eerdmans, 1995). See also Mark A. Noll, Nathan O. Hatch, and George M. Marsden, *The Search for Christian America,* expanded ed. (Colorado Springs, CO: Helmers & Howard, 1989); and Mark A. Noll, *The Scandal of the Evangelical Mind* (Grand Rapids: Eerdmans, 1995).

16. James N. Gregory, *American Exodus: The Dust Bowl Migration and Okie Culture in California* (New York: Oxford University Press, 1991), 193.

17. I refer to the Presbyterian Church (U.S.A.) and the Evangelical Lutheran Church of America, and not to conservative evangelical offshoots of these denominations.

18. These developments, not just in the Democratic Party but in other centers of power, account for the close political and social affinity shared by many evangelicals and Roman Catholics in early-twenty-first-century America. Evangelicals and Catholics remained deeply suspicious of one another well through John F. Kennedy's presidential campaign. The degree of cultural and even theological affinity they enjoy today would have been unimaginable into the 1980s. Consider the flourishing of the organization Evangelicals and Catholics Together (launched in 1992), and see Mark A. Noll and Carolyn Nystrom, *Is the Reformation Over? An Evangelical Assessment of Contemporary Roman Catholicism* (Grand Rapids: Baker Academic, 2005).

19. See Mark Stricherz, "Goodbye, Catholics: How One Man Reshaped the Democratic Party," *Commonweal*, November 4, 2005; www.commonwealmagazine .org/print_format.php?id_article=1422, accessed August 3, 2006.

20. See Louis Bolce and Gerald De Maio, "Our Secularist Democratic Party," *Public Interest*, Fall 2002; www.findarticles.com/p/articles/mi_m0377/is_2002_Fall/ ai_ 91972733/print, accessed August 3, 2006.

21. Stricherz, "Goodbye, Catholics."

22. Michael J. Gorman, "Ahead to Our Past: Abortion and Christian Texts," in *The Church and Abortion: In Search of a New Ground for Response,* ed. Paul T. Stallsworth (Nashville: Abingdon Press, 1993), 25–43.

23. Quoted in Chris Willman, *Rednecks and Bluenecks: The Politics of Country Music* (New York: The New Press, 2005), 108–9.

24. Charles Marsh, *The Beloved Community: How Faith Shapes Social Justice, From the Civil Rights Movement to Today* (New York: Basic Books, 2005), 143–44.

25. Quoted in Stephenie Hendricks, *Divine Destruction: Wise Use, Dominion Theology, and the Making of American Environmental Policy* (Hoboken, NJ: Melville House Publishers, 2005), 45.

26. Here I am in haste to note that Kennedy is a practicing Catholic and not a professed secularist. I do not question his own religious commitment, but suspect he has in his estimation of "fundamentalist" activism succumbed to the secularist tendency to subordinate faith and any reality that is the object of faith.

27. Hear it at Jerry Lee Lewis, *Live at the Star-Club Hamburg,* Bear Family Records, BCD 15467.

28. For the theological argument between Phillips and Lewis, hear "Religious Discussion," on *Jerry Lee Lewis: A Half Century of Hits,* Time-Life M19232. And consult Greil Marcus, *Mystery Train: Images of America in Rock 'n' Roll Music,* fourth revised edition (New York: Penguin Books, 1997), 290–93.

29. Michael Eric Dyson, *Mercy, Mercy Me: The Art, Loves, and Demons of Marvin Gaye* (New York: Basic Books, 2004), 108 and 122.

30. Christopher Lasch, *The Revolt of the Elites and the Betrayal of Democracy* (New York: W. W. Norton & Co., 1995), 16.

31. Johnny Cash with Patrick Carr, *Johnny Cash: The Autobiography* (New York: Harper Paperbacks, 1997), 271, 56.

32. Nick Lowe, "The Beast in Me" (Plangent Visions Music Inc.), from Johnny Cash, *American Recordings,* American 9 45520-2.

33. J.R. Cash, "A Half a Mile a Day" (no further publishing information provided); on *Johnny Cash: Personal File,* Columbia/Legacy 82796 94265 2.

CHAPTER 4: TRADITION AND PROGRESS

1. Oliver O'Donovan, *The Desire of the Nations* (Cambridge: Cambridge University Press, 1996), 244.

2. G. K. Chesterton, *What I Saw in America,* in *G. K. Chesterton: Collected Works,* vol. 21 (San Francisco: Ignatius Press, 1990), 85 and 171. In real and figurative senses, Chesterton as an acute European observer of American mores followed in the steps of his nineteenth-century French predecessor, Alexis de Tocqueville. Chesterton nowhere explicitly cites Tocqueville, but his ruminations, especially on America's fascination with the future and with progress, echo Tocqueville's so clearly that it appears quite likely he read and absorbed Tocqueville's masterwork *Democracy in America.* For instance, compare the quotation cited above, about New Yorkers digging up the foundations of a building just as the roof tiles are being installed, to this from Tocqueville: "In the United States, a man carefully builds a dwelling in which to pass his declining years, and he sells it while the roof is being laid; he plants a garden and rents it out just as he was going to taste its fruits. . . . Death finally comes, and stops him before he has grown weary of this useless pursuit of a complete felicity that always flees from him. One is at first astonished to contemplate the singular agitation displayed by so many happy men in the very midst of their abundance" (*Democracy in America,* trans. and ed. Harvey C. Mansfield and Delba Winthrop [Chicago: University of Chicago Press, 2000], II 2.13, 512).

3. Steve Turner, *The Man Called Cash: The Authorized Biography* (Nashville: W Publishing Group, 2004), 13.

4. *Ring of Fire: The Johnny Cash Reader,* ed. Michael Streissguth (Cambridge, MA: Da Capo Press, 2002), 23.

5. Michael Streissguth, *Johnny Cash: The Biography* (Cambridge, MA: Da Capo Press, 2006), 33.

6. On the topics of this paragraph, see especially Streissguth, *Johnny Cash: The Biography;* and Michael Streissguth, *Johnny Cash at Folsom Prison: The Making of a Masterpiece* (New York: Da Capo Press, 2004).

7. Rebecca Solnit, *River of Shadows: Eadweard Muybridge and the Technological Wild West* (New York: Penguin Books, 2003), 10.

8. Ibid., 9.

9. Mark Twain, *The Innocents Abroad* (New York: Harper & Row, 1911), vol. 2, chap. 31 (p. 386). The jocular Twain did not authorize this claim too vigorously,

feeling compelled to add a footnote: "Stated to me for a fact. I only tell it as I got it. I am willing to believe it. I can believe anything."

10. Floyd Jenkins, "Fireball Mail" (no further publishing information provided); A. P. Carter, "Wabash Cannonball" (no further publishing information provided); both found on Roy Acuff, *The Essential Roy Acuff: 1936–1949,* Columbia/Legacy CK 48956. Beasley Smith, "Tennessee Central (Number 9)," also recorded by Acuff, has lyrics included in Dorothy Horstman, *Sing Your Heart Out, Country Boy* (Nashville: Country Music Foundation Press, 1975), 373–74.

11. Johnny Cash, "Folsom Prison Blues" (no further publishing information provided), found on Johnny Cash, *The Sun Years,* Sun/Rhino R2 70950. For African Americans, the freedom symbolized by trains was substantial. Railways penetrated slave country in the 1830s and 1840s, but slaves were shackled in place. No wonder the liberating conveyor guiding escaped slaves north was known as the Underground Railroad. Before and certainly after emancipation, train travel provided what Angela Davis calls the African American's "most tangible evidence of freedom." See her *Blues Legacies and Black Feminism: Gertrude "Ma" Rainey, Bessie Smith, and Billie Holiday* (New York: Pantheon Books, 1998), 67, and our earlier mention of this factor in chapter 2.

12. Hank Snow, "Movin' On," found on various compilations, and covered by Cash, Elvis Presley, and many others.

13. Traditional, "Freight Train Blues," found on *The Essential Roy Acuff: 1936–1949.*

14. Jimmie Rodgers, "Brakeman's Blues" (no further publishing information provided), on Jimmie Rodgers, *First Sessions, 1927–1928,* Rounder CD 1056.

15. Joseph Needleman, cited in Ephraim Radner and Philip Turner, *The Fate of Communion: The Agony of Anglicanism and the Future of a Global Church* (Grand Rapids: Eerdmans, 2006), 31.

16. Christopher Lasch, *The True and Only Heaven: Progress and Its Critics* (New York: W. W. Norton & Co., 1991), 14.

17. See Solnit, *River of Shadows,* 62–63, 67; quotation 64–65.

18. C. Vann Woodward, *Origins of the New South: 1877–1913* (Baton Rouge: Louisana State University Press, 1951), 4–5, 117–18, and 379, quotations 7 and 379.

19. Quotation, Solnit, *River of Shadows,* 61; see also 59–62, and Marco d'Eramo, *The Pig and the Skyscraper: Chicago: A History of Our Future,* trans. Graeme Thomson (London: Verso, 2002), 17–18.

20. D'Eramo, *The Pig and the Skyscraper,* 45–46.

21. Traditional, "The Legend of John Henry." For Cash's 8:24 version, hear Johnny Cash, *Blood, Sweat and Tears,* Columbia/Legacy CK 66508.

22. See "Tracing the Roots of the Song 'John Henry' and Its Enduring Appeal," National Public Radio transcript from September 2, 2002, broadcast; accessed at www.npr.org February 7, 2007.

23. Jenkins (no first name provided), "Ben Dewberry's Final Run" (no further publishing information provided); found on Jimmie Rodgers, *First Sessions.*

24. Borrowing a basically identical line from "Casey Jones"—"we're going to reach Frisco but we'll be dead."

25. The denial of social dynamics was congruent with the American tendency to minimize or eliminate state regulation. The privately operated railroads of the United States were substantially more dangerous than their European state-run counterparts. According to d'Eramo, from 1898 to 1903, nineteen of every million railroad passengers in the United States died in train accidents. During the same period, Austria's railroad passenger mortality rate was 0.99 for every million—one-twentieth the American death rate. See d'Eramo, *The Pig and the Skyscraper,* 19.

26. J. Cash (credited), "Casey Jones" (no further publishing information provided); found on Johnny Cash, *Blood, Sweat and Tears.* J. Cash, B. Johnson, N. Blake, arrangement, "Wreck of the Old 97," no further publishing information provided; found on Johnny Cash, *At San Quentin,* Columbia/Legacy CK 66017. A. P. Carter, M. Carter, S. Carter, "Engine 143," no further publishing information provided; found on Johnny Cash, *Orange Blossom Special,* Columbia/Legacy, CK 86329.

27. Malone, quoted in Chris Willman, *Rednecks and Bluenecks: The Politics of Country Music* (New York: New Press, 2005), 12.

28. Elizabeth Fox-Genovese and Eugene D. Genovese, *The Mind of the Master Class: History and Faith in the Slaveholder's Worldview* (New York: Cambridge University Press, 2005), 2. See also d'Eramo, *The Pig and the Skyscraper,* 99–100.

29. I was first acquainted with this song through Uncle Tupelo's great acoustic album, *March 16–20, 1992,* Rockville, ROCK6090-2, which credits the piece as "traditional." More precise information on this song, Gunning, and her life may be found at dlib.nyu.edu/dram/objd/7569 (accessed January 31, 2007).

30. John Prine, "Paradise," no further publishing information provided; recorded by Cash on Johnny Cash, *Personal File,* Columbia/Legacy 82796 94265 2.

31. Lasch, *The True and Only Heaven,* 22–23.

32. Chesterton, *What I Saw in America,* 218.

33. Modernity and progress, with all their emphasis on the future, ironically now are unmasked for their chronological parochialism, not only in regard to the past, but to the future as well. With its relentless expectation of a ceaselessly expanding economy, modern progress burns up fossil fuels and other nonrenewable resources at astonishing rates. A *sustainable* economy by definition looks to the future and includes posterity. The nonsustainable economy of modern progressivism consumes with an eye only on the present. "Instant gratification" offers no incentive to care about great-grandchildren. More ominously, progress has brought technology on a scale that now can (through nuclear weaponry or catastrophic climate change) destroy the world. It is all too conceivable that humanity might be annihilated or practically returned to the Stone Age within this century. If, God forbid, anything of the kind occurs, then modern progress will have to be understood (if any are around to understand it) as a gigantically reckless, selfish, and arrogant burst of human ingenuity that finally resulted in overwhelming disaster. In such a case, the advances, goods, and comforts to the affluent masses, enjoyed in modernity as in no other age, will represent only a few centuries of (mixed) gain and comfort—at obliterating cost to ancestry and posterity. In other words, the jury is still out on whether or not progress is a historical success.

34. The "prosperity gospel" so ascendant especially in evangelicalism, and evidenced quite broadly in the popularity of such books as Joel Osteen's *Your Best Life Now* and Bruce Wilkinson's *The Prayer of Jabez*, is especially pernicious in this regard. Identifying material wealth with God's blessings, it not only puts God's grace at the service of those lucky enough to achieve affluence but endorses the perception that the impoverished are the "deserving poor"—too wicked or too dumb to avail themselves of God's blessings. Such attitudes occlude the witness of earlier American evangelicals, themselves much more in touch with the church's venerable traditions on wealth and poverty. Consider William Jennings Bryan, who was in fact more concerned about the effects of social Darwinism than of biological evolution. Consider the southern Presbyterian evangelical theologian Robert L. Dabney, who in the 1880s was among those critics who linked plutocracy with communism and expressed wariness of "free enterprise." See Michael Kazin, *A Godly Hero: The Life of William Jennings Bryan* (New York: Alfred A. Knopf, 2006), 140, 273–75, 289–95); Woodward, *Origins of the New South,* 173–74; as well as Donald W. Dayton, *Discovering an Evangelical Heritage* (New York: Harper & Row, 1976), and Genovese and Genovese, *Mind of the Master Class,* 649–79.

35. Alasdair MacIntyre's famous formulation in his *After Virtue: A Study in Moral Theory,* 2nd ed. (Notre Dame, IN: University of Notre Dame Press, 1984).

36. George Orwell, "The Lion and the Unicorn: Socialism and the English Genius," in *Essays* (New York: Everyman's Library, 2002), 348.

37. In Chesterton's much-repeated phrase, G. K. Chesterton, *Orthodoxy* (Garden City, NY: Image Books, 1959), 48.

CHAPTER 5: GUILT AND INNOCENCE

1. Michael Streissguth, *Johnny Cash: The Biography* (Cambridge, MA: Da Capo Press, 2006), 3.

2. Ibid., 4.

3. *Ring of Fire: The Johnny Cash Reader,* ed. Michael Streissguth (Cambridge, MA: Da Capo Press, 2002), 30.

4. Streissguth, *Ring of Fire,* 233.

5. Johnny Cash, with Patrick Carr, *Johnny Cash: The Autobiography* (New York: Harper Paperbacks, 1997), 39.

6. Richard T. Hughes, *Myths America Lives By* (Urbana and Chicago: University of Illinois Press, 2003), 164.

7. See Hughes, *Myths,* 53–189; and Andrew J. Bacevich, *The New American Militarism: How Americans Are Seduced by War* (New York: Oxford University Press, 2005), 11–12. See also Bacevich, *American Empire: The Realities of Consequences of U.S. Diplomacy* (Cambridge, MA: Harvard University Press, 2002). For a critique of President Bush's biblical interpretation and quotation, see Stephen B. Chapman, "Imperial Exegesis: When Caesar Interprets Scripture," in *Anxious about Empire: Theological Essays on the New Global Realities,* ed. Wes Avram (Grand Rapids: Brazos Press, 2004), 91–102.

8. Cornel West, *Democracy Matters: Winning the Fight against Imperialism* (New York: Penguin, 2004), 41.

9. See Allen Dwight Callahan, *The Talking Book: African Americans and the Bible* (New Haven, CT: Yale University Press, 2006), 25.

10. Elizabeth Fox-Genovese and Eugene D. Genovese, *The Mind of the Master Class: History and Faith in the Southern Slaveholder's Worldview* (New York: Cambridge University Press, 2005), 1.

11. The literature on black American history, if too usually and often unread, is voluminous. An excellent starting place remains Lerone Bennett Jr.'s compelling *Before the Mayflower,* issued in almost countless editions since its original publication in 1962. The edition on my bookshelf is *Before the Mayflower: A History of the Negro in America 1619–1964* (New York: Penguin Books, 1964); the latest is the New Millennium Edition, released in 2003.

12. See Rodney Clapp, "When Tulsa Burned: A Forgotten Episode in American Terrorism," *Books and Culture,* September/October 2002, 34–37. And for Springfield's 1908 attack on its black citizenry, see Jim Rasenberger, "Barack Obama and the Springfield Race Riot," *Salon.com,* February 10, 2007; accessed on February 15, 2007, at www.salon.com/opinion/feature/2007/02/10/obama_springfield/index.html. In 1919 alone, major race riots (with white invasion of black communities) occurred in Chicago, Charleston, Long View (Texas), Washington, DC, Knoxville, and Omaha. See Richard Hofstadter and Michael Wallace, eds., *American Violence: A Documentary History* (New York: Alfred A. Knopf, 1970), 246.

13. Patrick J. Deneen, *Democratic Faith* (Princeton, NJ: Princeton University Press, 2005), 116.

14. Quoted in Callahan, *The Talking Book,* xiv.

15. Howard Thurman, *Jesus and the Disinherited* (Boston: Beacon Press, 1976), 11–12; earlier quotations 18 and 29.

16. W. J. Cash, *The Mind of the South* (New York: Vintage Books, 1941, 1991), 86.

17. Robertson later sold The Family Channel to Fox; eventually Fox turned it over to ABC/Disney, where the network now resides as ABC Family. There are now no westerns on the network's schedule, though I presume that is not what is meant by the current tagline, "A New Kind of Family." See abcfamily.go.com.home.html, accessed February 26, 2007.

18. I can think of three possible exceptions: *The Roy Rogers Show* (1951–64), whose eponymous hero kept his (third) wife, Dale Evans, by his side both on and off camera; *Daniel Boone* (1964–70), which, set in Kentucky, would not strictly qualify as a western; and *Little House on the Prairie,* which also was not set in the Old West and did not premiere until 1974 (and ran until 1983).

19. *Shane,* directed by George Stevens (Paramount Pictures, 1953). Though he makes no comment on scapegoating per se, Richard Slotkin in his classic study of American violence recognizes that the hunter/killer master of American wilderness mythology is one who departs "the familial universe of order and safety" for the dangers and attractions of the frontier. This in itself calls into question the values of the "familial universe," suggesting "that the lure of the unknown and the forbidden has

more appeal" for the hunter/killer than the affections of settled society and domesticity. Slotkin notes that the hunter's "final atonement with society may take the form of a voluntary exile" and cites the earliest literary example of such exile as James Fenimore Cooper's *The Pioneers,* first published in 1823. See Richard Slotkin, *Regeneration through Violence: The Mythology of the American Frontier, 1600–1800* (Middletown, CT: Wesleyan University Press, 1973), 551 and 563–64.

20. *The Searchers,* directed by John Ford (C. V. Whitney Pictures, 1956).

21. Garry Wills, *John Wayne's America: The Politics of Celebrity* (New York: Simon & Schuster, 1997), 302. The myth of innocence and the murky dynamics of scapegoating may also help to explain another peculiarity of American heroism: why it is that twentieth-century American superheroes are masked or disguised when they are in the role of the "killer cleansing the world of things that 'need killing.' " Superman, Batman, Spider-Man, Captain America, Supergirl, the Green Lantern, and a host of other popular superheroes can dwell in ordinary American society only in the guise of their domesticated alter egos (Clark Kent, Bruce Wayne, Peter Parker, and so on). In their identity as costumed superheroes, they appear only violently to purge innocent society of evil, then disappear until the next purge is necessary.

22. See Esther Kaplan, *With God on Their Side* (New York: New Press, 2004), 149–66, quotation 165.

23. Informed readers will recognize Girardian inflections in this paragraph. I do not believe the termination of scapegoating is the only or singularly important consequence of Christ's atoning death. I do think René Girard and many following him have made compelling arguments that the witness of Jesus Christ reveals and effectively ends the pernicious dynamics of scapegoating. For the core of Girard's theory, see *The Girard Reader,* ed. James G. Williams (New York: Crossroad Publishing, 1996). For the best theological rendering of Girard's thought, see S. Mark Heim, *Saved from Sacrifice: A Theology of the Cross* (Grand Rapids: Eerdmans, 2006).

24. Philip Rieff, *Charisma: The Gift of Grace, and How It Has Been Taken Away from Us* (New York: Pantheon Books, 2007), 27, 218 (emphasis added). Rieff's statements on guilt are more polemical and rhetorically insistent. He calls guilt "the" (not "a") "main mechanism" in the making of covenant. I would argue that the main mechanism or central reality of covenant is God's gracious and precedent action toward and for creation. God's redemptive covenant with Israel *begins* with God's liberation of the people Israel from Egyptian slavery, not with the interdictory (and properly guilt-inducing) Ten Commandments.

25. Rieff, *Charisma,* 224.

26. Cash's overall sense of guilt was profoundly Christian, in that his conscience (sometimes accurately, sometimes inaccurately) spoke to him in the persona of a beloved brother. Though J.R./Johnny sometimes found Jack (his conscience) censorious, he never doubted that Jack fundamentally loved him and wished for him the best. Likewise, a biblically grounded and formed sense of guilt rests on a conviction that God first and foremost loves God's creatures. Divine censoriousness ultimately serves divine grace and human welfare.

27. Cash with Carr, *Autobiography,* 271.

28. Ibid., 56.

29. Streissguth, *Johnny Cash: The Biography,* 168.

30. Cash with Carr, *Autobiography,* 300.

31. Dan Flores, *Horizontal Yellow: Nature and History in the Near Southwest* (Albuquerque: University of New Mexico Press, 1999), 15–25.

32. Ibid., 23.

33. Charles C. Mann, *1491: New Revelations of the Americas before Columbus* (New York: Alfred A. Knopf, 2005), 9. Mann's book is an intelligent journalist's absorbing—and extremely sobering—account of the revised estimates of Native American populations and cultures arising from recently developed disciplines and technologies, such as climatology, pollen analysis, carbon-14 dating, and satellite photography (see 15).

34. Johnny Cash, *Bitter Tears: Ballads of the American Indian,* Columbia/ Legacy CK 66507. The songs from this album discussed below are Peter LaFarge, "As Long as the Grass Shall Grow"; LaFarge, "The Ballad of Ira Hayes"; LaFarge, "Custer"; J. Cash, "Apache Tears"; and J. Horton, "The Vanishing Race" (no further publishing information provided in all cases).

35. The actually historic story of Ira Hayes was later retold in Clint Eastwood's 2006 film, *Flags of Our Fathers.*

36. Reinhold Niebuhr, *The Irony of American History* (New York: Charles Scribner's Sons, 1952), 63.

CHAPTER 6: VIOLENCE AND PEACE

1. John Bakeless, *Daniel Boone: Master of the Wilderness* (New York: William Morrow & Co., 1939), 162.

2. See John Mack Faragher, *Daniel Boone: The Life and Legend of an American Pioneer* (New York: Henry Holt & Co., 1992), 17, 23, quotation 39. See also Bakeless, *Daniel Boone,* 1–14. For a vivid novelization of Quaker venturing into the northern U.S. and southern Canadian lands of the early nineteenth century, see Margaret Elphinstone, *The Voyageurs* (Edinburgh: Canongate, 2003).

3. Alexis de Tocqueville described Jackson as "a man of violent character and middling capacity," elected to the presidency on the dubious basis of overblown military exploits. See Tocqueville, *Democracy in America,* trans. Harvey C. Mansfield and Delba Winthrop (Chicago: University of Chicago Press, 2000), I 2.9 (p. 265).

4. Richard Slotkin, *Regeneration through Violence: The Mythology of the American Frontier, 1600–1800* (Middletown, CT: Wesleyan University Press, 1973), 269.

5. See Faragher, *Daniel Boone,* 334–35.

6. Slotkin, *Regeneration through Violence,* 414 and 555.

7. J. Cash, "Folsom Prison Blues," no further publishing information provided. The rousing live version is found at Johnny Cash, *At Folsom Prison,* Columbia/Legacy CK 65955.

8. *Ring of Fire: The Johnny Cash Reader,* ed. Michael Streissguth (Cambridge, MA: Da Capo Press, 2002), 218.

9. Steve Turner, *The Man Called Cash: The Authorized Biography* (Nashville:

W Publishing Group, 2004), 38, 83, 84, 89, 112. Michael Streissguth, *Johnny Cash: The Biography* (Cambridge, MA: Da Capo Press, 2006), 86. Nicholas Dawidoff, *In the Country of Country: People and Places in American Music* (New York: Pantheon Books, 1997), Jennings quotation, 188–89.

10. See Michael Streissguth, *Johnny Cash at Folsom Prison: The Making of a Masterpiece* (Cambridge, MA: Da Capo Books, 2004).

11. Sting, "I Hung My Head" (EMI Blackwood Music); from Johnny Cash, *American IV: The Man Comes Around,* American 440 063 339 2.

12. Johnny Cash, "The Big Battle," no further publishing information provided; from Johnny Cash, *America,* Columbia/Legacy CK 86260.

13. John Howard Yoder, *The Politics of Jesus: Vicit Agnus Noster*, 2nd ed. (Grand Rapids: Eerdmans, 1994), 130–31; for an overview of several supporting biblical texts, see 112–33.

14. See William C. Placher, *Narratives of a Vulnerable God: Christ, Theology, and Scripture* (Louisville, KY: Westminster John Knox Press, 1994), 21; and Pope Benedict XVI, "On the Revolution of Love," an address in St. Peter's Square, February 18, 2007, found at www.ekklesiaproject.org/content/view/176/1/, accessed February 28, 2007.

15. See W. Eugene Hollon, *Frontier Violence: Another Look* (New York: Oxford University Press, 1974), 197–203.

16. Ibid., 202–3, 196.

17. For much of the substance of this paragraph I am indebted to James C. Juhnke and Carol M. Hunter, *The Missing Peace: The Search for Nonviolent Alternatives in United States History* (Kitchener, ON: Pandora Press, 2001), esp. 175–76 and 199; and Perry Bush, "Violence, Nonviolence, and the Search for Answers in History," in J. Denny Weaver and Gerald Biesecker-Mast, eds., *Teaching Peace: Nonviolence and the Liberal Arts* (Lanham, MD: Rowan & Littlefield, 2003), 83.

18. It is a measure of how dangerously far we have proceeded with the wedding of democracy and militaristic empire that Reinhold Niebuhr, the theological father of *realpolitik* and a figure often genuflected to by today's neoconservatives, flatly assumed that, "A democracy can not of course, engage in an explicit preventive war." (See Niebuhr, *The Irony of American History* [New York: Charles Scribner's Sons, 1952], 146–47.) Preventive or preemptive war, though a practice Niebuhr regarded as capitulation to "simple idealism," is of course a declared doctrine of the American war on terror. The central document propounding the "Bush Doctrine," including preventive war, is the White House–issued *The National Security Strategy of the United States,* published September 17, 2002, and widely available, including in Wes Avram, ed., *Anxious about Empire: Theological Essays on the New Global Realities* (Grand Rapids: Brazos Press, 2004), 187–215. The literature on American empire is already massive and daily proliferating, but I will mention three books I have found especially illuminating on the subject: Chalmers Johnson, *Nemesis: The Last Days of the American Republic* (New York: Metropolitan Books, 2006); Michael Mann, *Incoherent Empire* (London: Verso, 2003); and Gary Dorrien, *Imperial Designs: Neoconservatism and the New Pax Americana* (New York: Routledge, 2004).

19. Elizabeth Fox-Genovese and Eugene D. Genovese, *The Mind of the Master Class* (New York: Cambridge University Press, 2005), 337 (quotation), 354–358. It is surely also germane that medieval knights "lived off violence and plunder" (355).

20. W. J. Cash, *The Mind of the South* (New York: Vintage Books, 1941, 1991), 73.

21. South Carolina governor John Lyde Wilson, *The Code of Honor,* quoted in Fox Butterfield, *All God's Children: The Bosket Family and the American Tradition of Violence* (New York: Avon Books: 1995, 1996), 12.

22. C. Vann Woodward, *Origins of the New South: 1887–1913* (Baton Rouge: Louisiana State University, 1951), 158.

23. See Robert M. Utley, *Billy the Kid: A Short and Violent Life* (Lincoln: University of Nebraska Press, 1989), 4.

24. See the extraordinary account by Butterfield, *All God's Children.*

25. Alexis de Tocqueville, *Democracy in America,* trans. and ed. Harvey C. Mansfield and Delba Winthrop (Chicago: University of Chicago Press, 2000), I.2.9, p. 267–68; I.1.1., p. 22.

26. Both quotes thus far in this paragraph are from Slotkin, *Regeneration through Violence,* 539. I am indebted to Slotkin's entire discussion of *Moby-Dick,* 538–50.

27. Herman Melville, *Moby-Dick, or, The Whale* (New York: The Modern Library, 2000). For this paragraph, chap. 14, p. 93; chap. 42, p. 281; chap. 48, p. 327; chap. 114, pp. 703–4; chap. 97, p. 613; chap. 88, p. 569; chap. 36, p. 328.

28. Ibid., chap. 66, p. 436; chap. 16, p. 101; chap. 57, p. 393; chap. 3, p. 34.

29. Rockwell Kent, whose illustrations were introduced with the 1930 edition of the novel, unmistakably depicts the fowl as a bald eagle. See p. 822 of the Modern Library edition.

30. Quotations in this paragraph: Ibid., chap. 134, p. 797; chap. 16, p. 100; chap. 135, pp. 821–22.

31. Ibid., chap. 134, p. 804.

32. See Jonathan Schell, *The Unconquerable World: Power, Nonviolence, and the Will of the People* (New York: Henry Holt & Co., 2003), 98 and 339.

33. Ibid., 98.

34. Quoted in Stanley Hauerwas, *Against the Nations: War and Survival in a Liberal Society* (Minneapolis: Winston Press, 1985), 193.

35. See Juhnke and Hunter, *The Missing Peace,* 53, 60, 64.

36. See Ira Chernus, *American Nonviolence: The History of an Idea* (Maryknoll, NY: Orbis, 2004), x–xi, 44, 210–11.

37. Martin Luther King Jr., *A Testament of Hope: The Essential Writings of Martin Luther King, Jr.,* ed. James M. Washington (San Francisco: Harper & Row, 1986), 252.

CHAPTER 7: ON BAPTISM, PATRIOTISM, AND BEING A CHRISTIAN IN PUBLIC

1. George Orwell, "Notes on Nationalism," in *Essays* (New York: Everyman's Library, 1968), 866.

2. Randolph S. Bourne, "The State," in *War and the Intellectuals: Collected Essays 1915–1919* (Indianapolis: Hackett Publishing Co., 1964), 67–68.

3. Orwell, "The Lion and the Unicorn: Socialism and the English Genius," in *Essays*, 292.

4. Bourne, "The State," in *War and the Intellectuals*, 68; Orwell, "Notes on Nationalism," in *Essays*, 866.

5. Bourne, "The State," in *War and the Intellectuals*, 68. For Orwell on patriotism as "defensive," see "Notes on Nationalism," in *Essays*, 866.

6. Bourne, "The State," in *War and the Intellectuals*, 87.

7. Ibid., 74.

8. Orwell was not as wary of war as Bourne—for one thing, he had a more justifiable war to defend. But he refused to glorify war and saw it as a recourse that might on occasion be "necessary, but it is certainly not right or sane." See "Writers and Leviathan," in *Essays*, 1267.

9. Put differently, Christians should not practice or endorse "civil religion." We already have a religion. In a nontheocratic society of several religions, no god of the nation can be conceived that is not implicitly or explicitly other than the distinctive God of Israel, met in Christ. This is patently and unequivocally revealed in the legal arguments of the evangelically dominated Bush administration on behalf of retaining the phrase "under God" in the pledge of allegiance. See Rodney Clapp, "Hollow Pledge: The Problem with 'under God,' " *Christian Century*, November 16, 2004, 30–33.

10. The public, writes philosopher Jeffrey Stout, is addressed "whenever one addresses people as citizens." Any setting where citizens gather "as persons jointly responsible for the public good" is a "potentially public setting." Similarly, the political scientist Troy Dostert avers that "the public realm . . . [is] a site of shifting meanings and truth-claims," constantly mutating and never simply locatable as various communities bring their concerns into discussion. See Jeffrey Stout, *Democracy and Tradition* (Princeton, NJ: Princeton University Press, 2004), 113; and Troy Dostert, *Beyond Political Liberalism: Toward a Post-Secular Ethics of Public Life* (Notre Dame, IN: University of Notre Dame Press, 2006), 12.

11. Put metaphorically, this means Christians must be multilingual. The first and most comprehensive language for the Christian is that of Scripture and the Christian tradition. Christians should be free to speak of their specific Christian convictions and practices in various publics, and on behalf of or against certain governmental policies. (Of course, the same applies to those of other faiths and philosophies.) But in the democratic public, Christians do not speak in fiat or try to make the nation-state into a church. They must be ready and willing to articulate their reasons (theological and otherwise) on policies. They must furthermore be willing and able to argue how policies deriving from their convictions will work to the good of the American democracy, to the common good of the nation that is composed of people of many faiths and philosophies. This may often or even typically entail the ability to "translate" Christianly derived concerns into other "languages," showing how such concerns and policies will benefit all. (Or, in a tragic world, work to the greatest possible achievable common good.)

12. Karl Barth, *Church Dogmatics* IV/2, ed. G. W. Bromiley and T. F. Torrance, trans. G. W. Bromiley (Edinburgh: T. & T. Clark, 1958), 546 (emphasis added).

Select Discography

The following is not a comprehensive list of songs mentioned in the course of this book. It does include key songs representing the key themes of their respective chapters, and especially songs which receive some detailed attention.

All source/album listings are in compact disc format. The asterisk (*) preceding many entries indicates songs available on an iTunes iMix based on the themes of this book. The iMix can be located online at the iTunes store, under the title *Johnny Cash and America*.

CHAPTER 1: AMERICA'S SOUTHERN ACCENT

*Johnny Cash, "Southern Accents." *Unchained,* American 314 586 791-2.

*Tom T. Hall, "Me and Jesus." *We All Got Together and. . ./Storyteller,* Hux Records B000P0IM0A.

*Johnny Cash, "Down There by the Train." *American Recordings,* American 9 45520-2.

CHAPTER 2: LONESOMENESS AND COMMUNITY

*Hank Williams, "I'm So Lonesome I Could Cry." *24 of Hank Williams' Greatest Hits,* Mercury Nashville 823 293-2.

*Leonard Cohen and U2, "Tower of Song." *I'm Your Man: Motion Picture Soundtrack,* Verve Forecast B0007169-02.

*Johnny Cash, "Big River." *The Sun Years,* Sun/Rhino R2 70950.

*Big Bill Broonzy, "Goin' Down This Road Feeling Bad (Lonesome Road Blues)." *The Best of Big Bill Broonzy,* Blues Forever B00065TZP0.

*Merle Haggard, "White Line Fever." *Down Every Road,* Capitol-Nashville 7243-8-35713-2-1.

*Johnny Cash, "The Man Comes Around." *American IV: The Man Comes Around,* American 440063 339-2.

CHAPTER 3: HOLINESS AND HEDONISM

Jimmie Davis, "Red Nightgown Blues." *When the Sun Goes Down, Vol. 2: The First Time I Met the Blues,* Bluebird 09026-63987-2.

Jerry Lee Lewis, "Whole Lotta Shakin' Goin' On." *Live at the Star-Club Hamburg,* Bear Family Records BCD 15467.

Jerry Lee Lewis and Sam Phillips, "Religious Discussion." *A Half Century of Hits,* Time Life Records, M19232/OPCD-7863/B0005951-02.

*Marvin Gaye, "What's Going On." *What's Going On,* Motown 440 064 022-2.

CHAPTER 4: TRADITION AND PROGRESS

*Roy Acuff, "Wabash Cannonball." *The Essential Roy Acuff: 1936–1949,* Columbia/Legacy CK 48956.

*Johnny Cash, "Orange Blossom Special." *Orange Blossom Special.* Columbia/Legacy CK 86329.

*Jimmie Rodgers, "The Brakeman's Blues." *First Sessions, 1927–1928,* Rounder CD 1056.

*Johnny Cash, "The Legend of John Henry's Hammer." *Blood, Sweat and Tears,* Columbia/Legacy CK 66508.

*Johnny Cash, "Engine 143." *Orange Blossom Special,* Columbia/Legacy CK 86329.

*Johnny Cash, "The L & N Don't Stop Here Anymore." *Silver,* Columbia/Legacy CK 86791.

*John Prine, "Paradise." *John Prine,* Atlantic B000002I97.

CHAPTER 5: GUILT AND INNOCENCE

*Johnny Cash, "The Ballad of Ira Hayes." *Bitter Tears: Ballads of the American Indian,* Columbia/Legacy CK 66507.

*Johnny Cash, "Custer." *Bitter Tears: Ballads of the American Indian,* Columbia/Legacy CK 66507.

*Johnny Cash, "The Vanishing Race." *Bitter Tears: Ballads of the American Indian,* Columbia/Legacy CK 66507.

CHAPTER 6: VIOLENCE AND PEACE

*Johnny Cash, "Folsom Prison Blues." *At Folsom Prison,* Columbia/Legacy CK65955.

*Johnny Cash, "Delia's Gone." *American Recordings,* American 9 45520-2.

*Johnny Cash, "Cocaine Blues." *At Folsom Prison,* Columbia/Legacy CK65955.

*Johnny Cash, "The Big Battle." *America,* Columbia/Legacy CK 86260.

Index

155